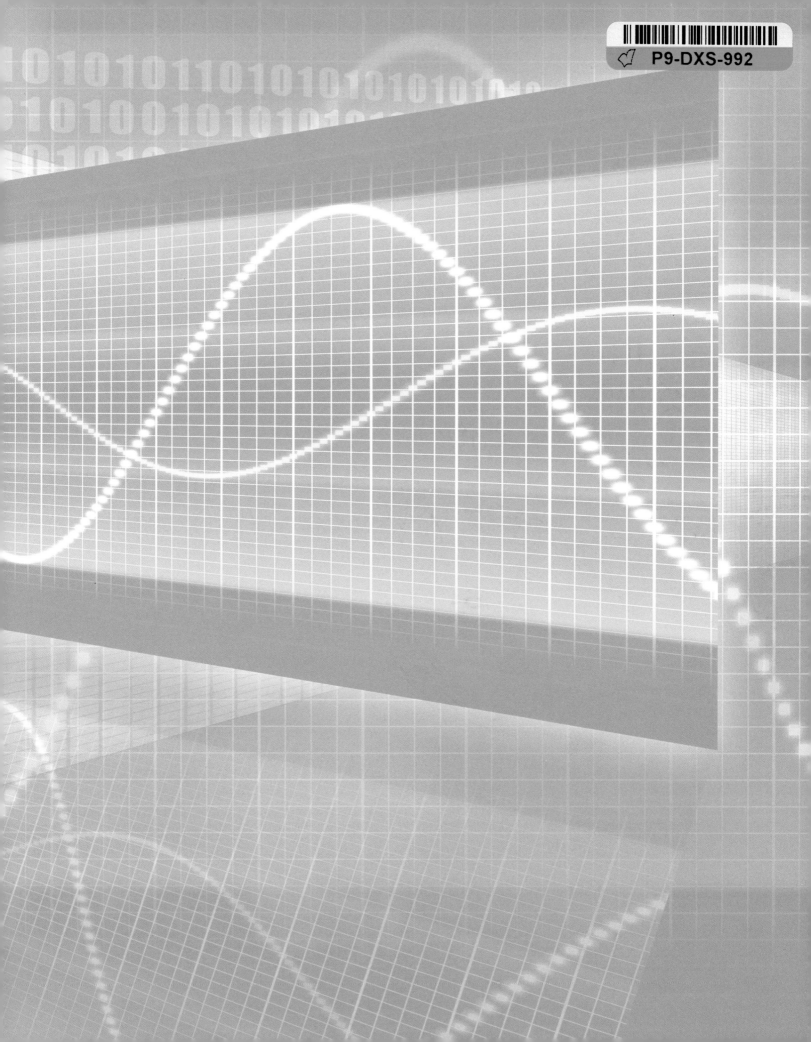

TIME
FOR KIDS

That's Awesome!

The World's Most Amazing Facts & Records!

TIME FOR KIDS
Managing Editor, TIME FOR KIDS: Nellie Gonzalez Cutler
Editor, Time Learning Ventures: Jonathan Rosenbloom

Book Packager: R studio T, New York
Art Direction/Design: Raúl Rodriguez and Rebecca Tachna
Writer: Lora Myers

TIME HOME ENTERTAINMENT INC.
Publisher: Richard Fraiman
General Manager: Steven Sandonato
Executive Director, Marketing Services: Carol Pittard
Director, Retail & Special Sales: Tom Mifsud
Director, New Product Development: Peter Harper
Director, Bookazine Development & Marketing: Laura Adam
Publishing Director, Brand Marketing: Joy Butts
Assistant General Counsel: Helen Wan
Design & Prepress Manager: Anne-Michelle Gallero
Book Production Manager: Susan Chodakiewicz
Associate Marketing Manager: Jonathan White
Associate Prepress Manager: Alex Voznesenskiy
Assistant Production Manager: Brynn Joyce

Special Thanks to: Christine Austin, Jeremy Biloon, Glenn Buonocore, Jim Childs, Rose Cirrincione, Jacqueline Fitzgerald, Carrie Frazier, Lauren Hall, Suzanne Janso, Raphael Joa, Mona Li, Robert Marasco, Amy Migliaccio, Kimberly Posa, Richard Prue, Brooke Reger, Dave Rozzelle, Ilene Schreider, Adriana Tierno, Sydney Webber, Time Imaging

For information on TIME For Kids magazine for the classroom or home, go to WWW.TFKCLASSROOM.COM or call 1-800-777-8600.

For subscriptions to Sports Illustrated for Kids, go to www.sikids.com or call 1-800-889-6007.

Published by Time Home Entertainment Inc.
Time Inc.
1271 Avenue of the Americas
New York, New York 10020

ISBN 10: 1-60320-156-4
ISBN 13: 978-1-60320-156-8
Library of Congress Control Number: 2010927616

"TIME for Kids" is a trademark of Time Inc.

We welcome your comments and suggestions about TIME for Kids Books. Please write to us at:
TIME for Kids Books
Attention: Book Editors
PO Box 11016
Des Moines, IA 50336-1016

If you would like to order any of our hardcover Collector's Edition books, please call us at 1-800-327-6388. (Monday through Friday, 7:00 a.m.– 8:00 p.m. or Saturday, 7:00 a.m.– 6:00 p.m. Central Time).

1TLF10

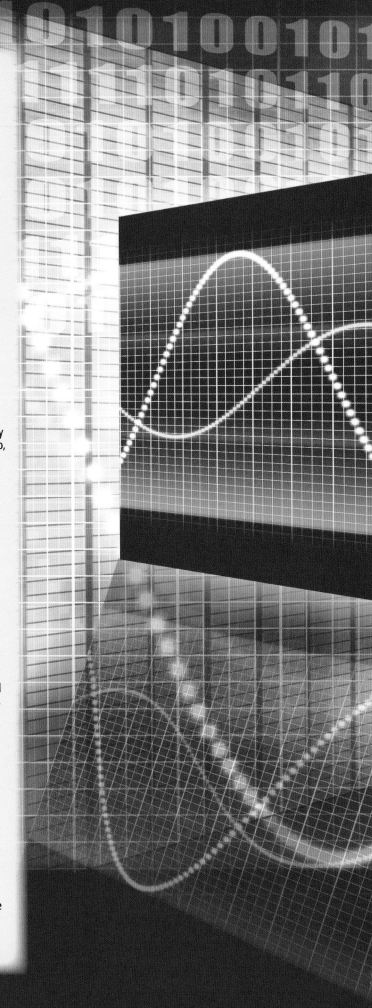

Contents

It's an Awesome World

Who won the gold for snowboarding in the 2010 Winter Olympics? See Awesome Sports.

Who was the first girl to play Little League baseball? Awesome History has the answer.

Who built a concert hall that looks like a shiny metal ship? Check out Awesome Arts.

Earth is a place of natural and human-made wonders. From a tiny gecko lizard, no larger than a thumbnail, to a lofty skyscraper that almost reaches the clouds, this book offers a glimpse of some of the most amazing, astonishing, and truly mind-boggling things to see, do, and experience on our planet. With every turn of the page you'll find incredible photos, fascinating facts, and amazing information that may surprise you. As you read this book, you will be saying:

"WOW! THAT'S AWESOME!"

Who enjoys snacking on grasshoppers? Go to Awesome Eats.

What's the fastest land animal on Earth? Zip over to Awesome Animals & Plants.

Where do people weave islands to live on? Travel to Awesome Earth.

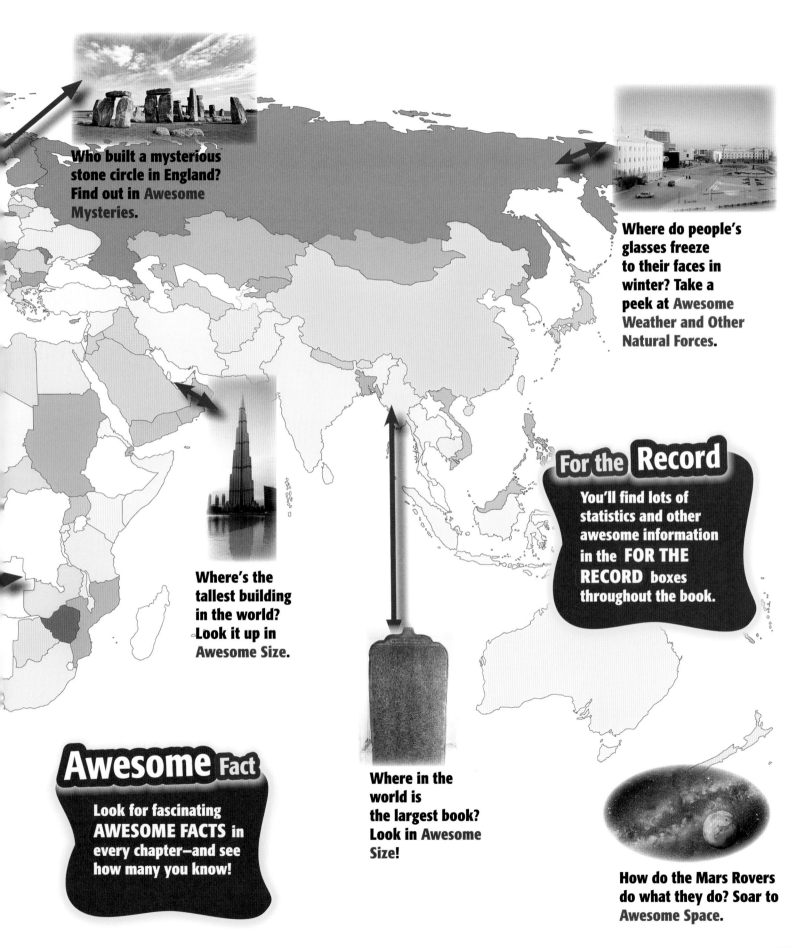

Who built a mysterious stone circle in England? Find out in Awesome Mysteries.

Where do people's glasses freeze to their faces in winter? Take a peek at Awesome Weather and Other Natural Forces.

For the Record

You'll find lots of statistics and other awesome information in the FOR THE RECORD boxes throughout the book.

Where's the tallest building in the world? Look it up in Awesome Size.

Awesome Fact

Look for fascinating AWESOME FACTS in every chapter—and see how many you know!

Where in the world is the largest book? Look in Awesome Size!

How do the Mars Rovers do what they do? Soar to Awesome Space.

Chapter 1

Awesome Size

For the Record

160 stories high, the world's tallest building (for now!) is the **BURJ KHALIFA**, located in the Middle East's Dubai, United Arab Emirates.

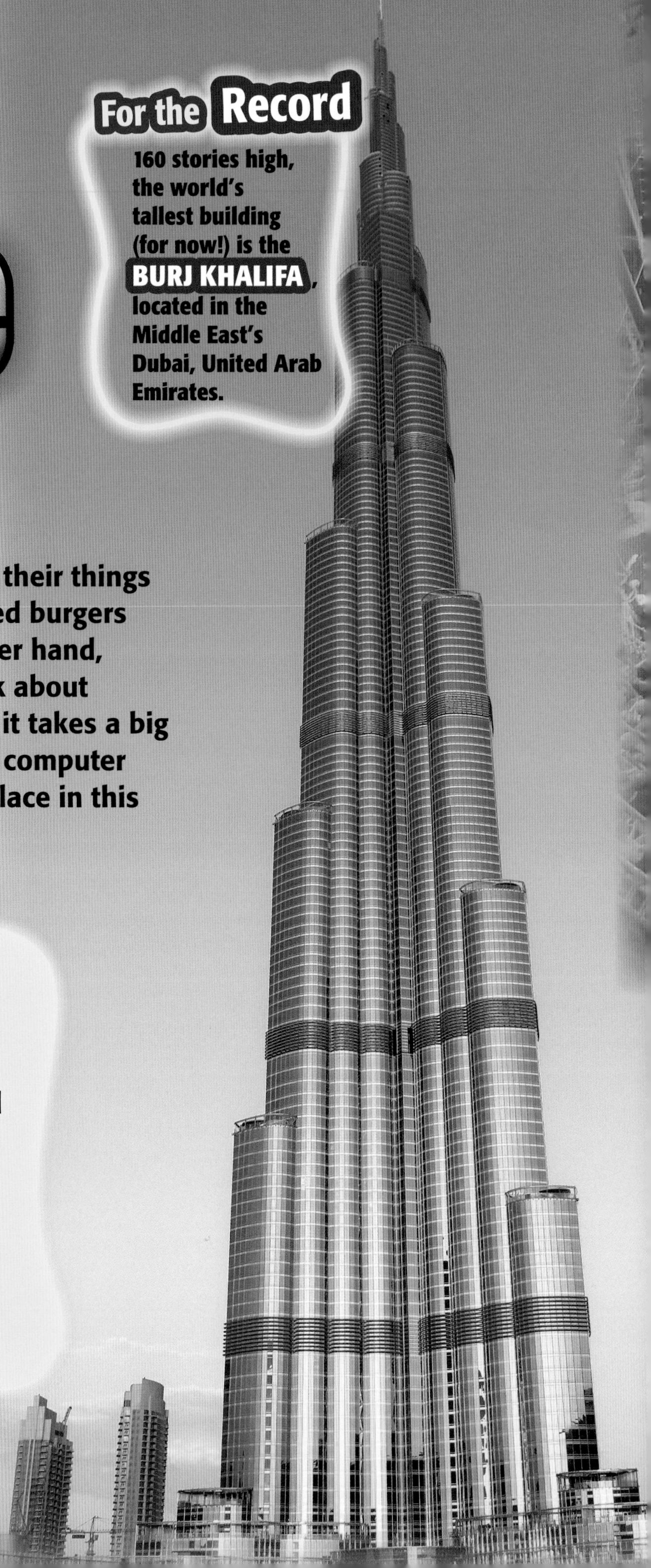

Sometimes it seems that humans like their things to be **REALLY, REALLY BIG**. Super-sized burgers and fries. Monster TV sets. On the other hand, **SMALL THINGS** are just as much fun. Think about iPods. Miniature golf. And sometimes it takes a big idea to create something small–like a computer chip! The moral is: every size has its place in this awesome world of ours.

In This Chapter

- Daunting Dinosaurs
- Dogs Big and Small
- The Largest Ferris Wheel
- The Smallest Gecko
- The Tallest Building
- The Biggest Little Circus on Earth
- And Much More…

Amazing Fact

The amazingly tiny **HOWARD BROTHERS CIRCUS** is made up of one million miniature pieces, all carved by one man.

Amazing Fact

A **DWARF GEKKO**, the world's smallest reptile, can easily fit on a finger and is about the size of a quarter.

Daunting Dinos

Thinking big? Think **DINOSAURS**—the most humongous creatures that ever walked the earth. The fossil remains of these mega-reptiles have been found on every continent except Antarctica.

Move Over, *T-Rex* !

Meat-eating **Spinosaurus** was about two tons heavier than *Tyrannosaurus Rex*, paleontologists say. Named for the jagged spines on their backs, Spinosaurs grew to be about 56 feet (17 m) long, and had muscular front arms with razor-sharp claws—the better to snatch their prey!

Awesome Fact

In the 2001 movie *Jurassic Park III*, *Spinosaurus* kills *Tyrannosaurus* after a heart-stopping battle. But scientists know this fight would be impossible. These giant reptiles lived in different parts of the planet during different pre-historic times!

Some Spinosaurs could be up to 5 times my height!

Deadly Deinonychus

Five feet tall and ten feet long, meat-eater *Deinonychus* (Die-*non*-ee-kuss) didn't size up to *Spinosaurus*. But it was just as mean a killing machine, and it could move like the wind on two bird-like legs. Its big brain cavity suggests that it could outsmart its victims!

Actual Size

TOP 5 Biggest Dinosaurs

	LENGTH (feet/meters)	WEIGHT (tons/metric tons)
1. Biggest Sauropod: *Argentinosaurus*	120 ft (36 m)	100 t (89 mt)
2. Biggest Carnivore: *Spinosaurus*	55 ft (16.5 m)	8 t (7 mt)
3. Biggest Pliosaur: *Liopleurodon*	50 ft (15 m)	30 t (27 mt)
4. Biggest Hadrosaur: *Shantungosaurus*	50 ft (15 m)	50 t (44.5 mt)
5. Biggest Raptor: *Utahraptor*	20 ft (6 m)	1 t (0.9 mt)

Scaling Up

How big is big? It all depends. To a small lizard, a garden snake looks big. To a garden snake, an iguana looks big. To an iguana...well, you get the idea. In the reptile world, you'll find all sizes—from almost invisible to gigantic!

Which Is Bigger?

Slithering in the rain forests of South America, the **anaconda** holds the record for the biggest body mass, or weight— an average of 330 pounds (148.5 kg). Anacondas can grow as big around the middle as a grown man!

Awesome Facts

● Anacondas are sometimes called "water boas" because they live in rivers and swamps. They are carnivores, eating mostly fish and birds—or even larger animals, like goats, that happen to come the reptile's way.

● Anacondas keep growing their whole lives. The longest anaconda found to date was 37.5 feet (11.43 m) from head to the tip of his tail.

TOP 5 Longest Snakes*

1. **Reticulated python** 35 feet (105 m)
2. **Green anaconda** 28 feet (84 m)
3. **Indian python** 25 feet (75 m)
4. **Diamond python** 21 feet (63 m)
5. **King cobra** 19 feet (57 m)

5 (15) 10 (30) 15 (45) 20 (60) 25 (75) 30 (90) 35 (105)
feet (m)

* average size

Source: Top 10 Everything 2007, Octopus Publishing Group Ltd.

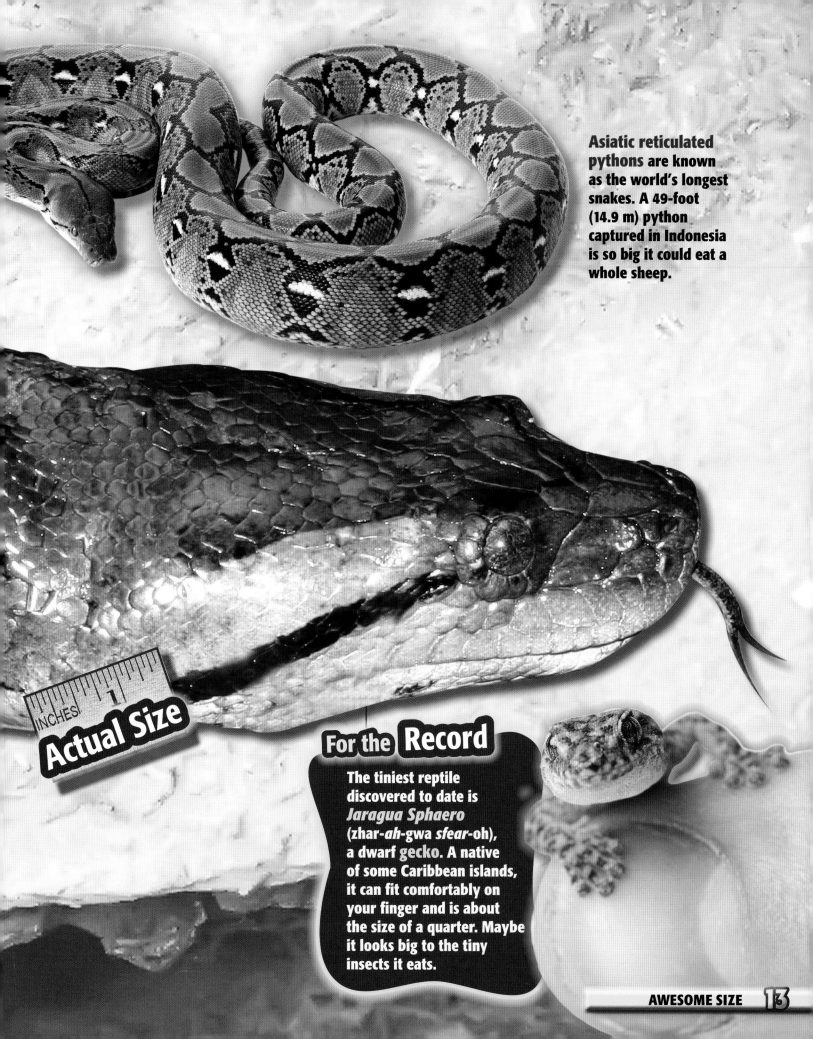

Asiatic reticulated pythons are known as the world's longest snakes. A 49-foot (14.9 m) python captured in Indonesia is so big it could eat a whole sheep.

INCHES 1

Actual Size

For the Record

The tiniest reptile discovered to date is *Jaragua Sphaero* (zhar-*ah*-gwa *sfear*-oh), a dwarf gecko. A native of some Caribbean islands, it can fit comfortably on your finger and is about the size of a quarter. Maybe it looks big to the tiny insects it eats.

Going to the Dogs

If you're longing for a **DOG**, first think about the size of your home. Do you have a small apartment or a big house with plenty of space outdoors? It's important to give some breeds room to roam. Luckily, there are lots of breeds to choose from—toy-sized to outsized!

Bouncy Bichons

Bichon Frise (Bee-shown free-say)

Fluffy, white, and cheerful, Bichons love to play and do tricks. But don't leave them home alone— they hate being apart from their owners for long.

> **Height to shoulder: up to 35 inches (88 cm)**
>
> **Weight: 100-120 pounds (45-54 kg)**

> **Height to shoulder: up to 11 inches (27 cm)**
>
> **Weight: 7-12 pounds (3-5.5 kg)**

Truly Great Dane

They're not called "great" for nothing! These big, powerful dogs are as friendly as they are huge.

Massive English Mastiff

Centuries ago, in Merry Old England, mastiffs were bred to be fighters. Today they are watchful protectors of their human owners.

> **Height to shoulder: up to 32 inches (80 cm)**
>
> **Weight: 150-200 pounds (68-91 kg)**

Gentle Irish Wolfhounds

While the wolfhound may tower over small children, owners say their sweet nature makes them perfect playmates.

Height to shoulder: up to 32 inches (80 cm)

Weight: 105-125 pounds (47-56 kg)

Height to shoulder: up to 9 inches (22 cm)

Weight: 3-6 pounds (1.5-2.7 kg)

Cheeky Chihuahuas

Chihuahua (Chee-*wah*-wah)

They're the world's smallest dogs—but they have super-sized personalities. Watch them stand up to dogs that are 10 times bigger!

INCHES 1

Actual Size

Reaching for the Sky

The ancient legend of the Tower of Babel tells us that humans have long dreamed of building structures that would touch the sky. All it took was a few thousand years to develop the know-how! Here is a look at some of the world's most awesome structures.

Blast from the Past

In 1981, a 26-year-old American, Dan Goodwin, climbed the outside of Willis Tower to the top, using suction cups and rock-climbing tools and wearing a Spider-Man costume. Although he was arrested for trespassing when he reached the top, Goodwin was later released.

Burj Khalifa
Dubai, United Arab Emirates

It opened in January 2010. It closed a month later for repairs. Officially, though, the **Burj Khalifa**, in the Middle Eastern emirate, or state, of Dubai, is now the world's tallest building. At **2,727 feet** (828 m) from the ground floor to the top of its antenna, it's almost twice the height of the Willis Tower.

The Burj Khalifa's observation deck is at Level 124—almost a half-mile up!

Just imagine the views from the tower's 1,044 apartments!

Willis Tower
Chicago, U.S.

The tallest skyscraper in the United States is **Willis Tower** (originally called Sears Tower). Completed in 1973, its official height is 1,451 feet (442 m)—but if you count the antenna on top, it reaches **1,730 feet** (527 m).

Empire State Building
New York City, U.S.

An impressive **1,453 feet, 8 9/16 inches** (443.2 m) from its base to the tip of its lightning rod, the Empire State Building is the tallest skyscraper in New York City. Completed in 1931, it became known throughout the world when King Kong climbed to the top in the classic 1933 movie.

Eiffel Tower
Paris, France

Want to get the best views of Paris, France? You can't do better than the observation decks in the **1,063-foot** (324 m) Eiffel Tower. Built by Gustave Eiffel as the entrance to the 1889 world's fair, it remains one of the greatest landmarks in the world.

NUMBER ONE IN THE RORLD

Washington Monument

Washington, D.C.

The white marble monument has the shape of an obelisk—a tall, narrow structure used by the ancient Egyptians. Completed in 1884 in honor of America's first president, it rises just over **555 feet** (169 m) above the National Mall and attracts about 24 million visitors each year.

Compared to these giants, you would be the size of the period at the end of this sentence.

NUMBER ONE IN THE U.S.

With 108 stories plus two rooftops, Willis Tower was once the tallest building in the world.

Circle of Thrills

For the biggest ride of your life, you can't beat the **SINGAPORE FLYER**. As of 2010, it holds the title as the world's largest giant observation wheel (what we call a Ferris wheel). It's named after the country where it is located—Singapore, an island nation in Southeast Asia.

Each of the 28 air-conditioned capsules is as big as a city bus and holds 28 passengers.

TOP 5
Biggest Ferris Wheels in the World

NAME	LOCATION	HEIGHT
1. Singapore Flyer	Singapore	542 feet (165 m)
2. Star of Nanchang	China	525 feet (160 m)
3. London Eye	Great Britain	427 feet (130 m)
4. Changsha	China	394 feet (120 m)
5. Southern Star	Australia	394 feet (120 m)

The Singapore Flyer rises 541 feet (165 m)—as tall as a 42-story building. The wheel's diameter is 494 ft (150 m).

It takes about 30 minutes for the wheel to go around once!

Riders on the Flyer get a spectacular 360-degree view of Singapore's Marina Bay.

Blast from the Past

The first Ferris wheel was 264 feet (80 m) high. An American bridge builder, George Washington Gale Ferris, Jr., designed the original ride in 1893 for the world's fair in Chicago, Illinois. When Ferris announced his plan to build it, skeptics laughed, calling him "the man who has wheels in his head." But the Ferris wheel was a huge success. It had 36 cars, each holding up to 60 people, and took 20 minutes to go around twice. The cost of a ticket: 50 cents!

Big Print, Small Print

Whether it's a thick novel or a slim volume of poems, a book's value is not measured by its size, but by the enjoyment it gives to the reader.

A Hard Book to Read

Want to curl up in bed with a good book? Sorry, but it won't be this one. Meet the **biggest book in the world**—and it's written in stone! You can find the book at the Kuthodaw Pagoda—a large temple in the city of Mandalay, in the Southeast Asian country of Burma (also known as Myanmar).

Awesome Facts

● Stone shrines on the temple grounds contain 729 "pages" of a whole Buddhist text. Each shrine holds one page—a **marble slab** with text on both sides.

● Carved by Buddhist monks, the marble book took almost nine years to complete. It was finished in 1869.

Micro-book

Bookmakers who work in miniature use microscopes, tiny tools, and light-weight paper that is easy to cut and to bind. The finished work contains the same text as the regular version of the book, but the words are written, printed, pressed, or engraved on a much smaller scale.

For the Record

A librarian in Cincinnati, Ohio, loves to collect miniature books. His volume of *Chameleon*, by the 19th-century Russian writer Anton Chekhov, is not much larger than a grain of salt.

This tiny speck is the actual book. It's smaller than the period at the end of this sentence.

This is a larger replica.

Tiny Technology

Many inventions start out big—and then shrink down to size. There were grandfather clocks long before there were wristwatches. The first computers took up entire rooms. But now many inventors think **SMALL AND COMPACT**—from cameras to cell phones—are the way to go.

Pint-Sized Phone

Want to make small talk? Good timing: Cell phones are getting **smaller** and **lighter**. There are many new models that are a tad over 3 inches long (7.6cm) and weigh about 3 ounces (85g). In some of the best mini-phones, new types of microchips make it easier to hear the person talking to you.

Built for a Doll

Television sets are getting bigger and wider—except for this model. A British company sells **a tiny working TV** with a 2-inch (5.1 cm) screen—a perfect fit in a dollhouse living room or to hold in the palm of your hand. But the $200 price is definitely full-size! And it doesn't even come with a remote!

Seeing Is Videotaping

Listen up, James Bond! The modern spy can now come out of the shadows and take secret videos in full daylight. A tiny video camera hidden in a pair of high-tech sunglasses captures, in color, whatever the wearer sees ahead. These glasses also come with clear lenses so the spy can also do his or her surveillance (and recording) indoors.

Micro-Worlds

Combine a microscope with a camera and click! You get a micrograph, a photo of an object that's invisible to the naked eye. Micrographs are useful in getting up-close views of tiny organisms and biologic forms. This one shows grains of minerals inside a thin section of limestone.

Warrior on a Mountaintop

When it's finished, it will be the world's largest mountain carving. The subject is **CRAZY HORSE** , a fearless Native American warrior in the 19th century. The sculpture will be bigger than Mount Rushmore, the famous American landmark that is located nearby.

In the Black Hills of South Dakota, sculptors and engineers have been working on the giant statue of Crazy Horse since 1948. Using carefully-controlled explosives, the team blasts the rock to carve out the stone. The memorial was designed by Korczak Ziolkowski (*core*-chock jewel-*cuff*-ski), a Polish-American artist who had worked briefly on the stone portraits of U.S. Presidents at Mount Rushmore.

This is how the monument will look when it is finished.

The head of Crazy Horse was completed in 1998. It is 87 feet (27 m) tall—27 feet (8 m) higher than the head of a U.S. President on Mount Rushmore. The finished statue will be 563 feet (172 m) high and 641 feet (195 m) wide. When will the memorial be completed? No one knows for sure.

Awesome Facts

● The son of a medicine man, Crazy Horse was born into a Lakota Sioux (lah-*koe*-tah *sue*) tribe in the Black Hills area of South Dakota around 1842.

● From 1823 to 1890, United States troops and groups of Indian tribes fought a series of wars for control of the West. Crazy Horse was a leader in many battles during the 1860s and 1870s. He was trying to protect the Sioux from U.S. soldiers who wanted to take the Native Americans' land, as well as from enemy tribes.

● In May of 1877, tired of fighting, Crazy Horse surrendered to the U.S. Cavalry. Several months later, while trying to escape from prison, he was killed by an army guard.

Seventeen miles from the Crazy Horse Memorial, the faces of four great U.S. Presidents are carved into the side of Mount Rushmore. Can you identify them?

Answer: (from left to right) George Washington, Thomas Jefferson, Theodore Roosevelt, Abraham Lincoln

It's a Small World, After All

Thanks to jet-speed air travel, instant messaging, and satellite TV, the world seems to be getting smaller. Some artists and designers who agree with that idea are taking it to the next level.

A Wee Place Called Home

Want a house of your very own? Jay Shafer at the **Tumbleweed Tiny House Company** may have one for you! In his office in San Francisco, California, Shafer draws up plans for homes that he says are smaller than some people's closets. In most of them there is room enough for a kitchen, a bathroom with a shower, and a living room where up to four people can hang out. Shafer's newest design is an 8-foot by 15-foot (2-m by 5-m) house on wheels that can be moved from city to countryside!

A small table and a shelf for cookbooks fit nicely in the kitchen.

From
TIME
FOR KIDS
Magazine

This miniature scene from *Alice in Wonderland* fits in the eye of a needle as does the tiny Statue of Liberty (below).

When Willard Wigan was five years old, he made a house for the ants in his backyard in Birmingham, England. "I felt sorry for them because I thought they were homeless," he told TFK. The tiny house was just the first of Wigan's miniature creations. Soon he was making tiny bicycles, furniture, even shoes. "It became an obsession," he says. "It started to take over my life." Today, Wigan's works are a lot more complicated. Even so, each one can fit inside the eye of a needle.

Wigan's sculptures may be the smallest manmade works of art in the world. He constructs them out of plastic bag ties under a microscope. He uses a small diamond attached to the point of a needle to shape the pieces. Then, he puts on paint with a hair plucked from a fly! Some of his sculptures can take up to four months to finish. All of his art is invisible to the naked eye. The pieces must be displayed in custom-built cases equipped with microscopes.

As a child, Wigan had learning disabilities. He struggled to get good grades. "I felt small," he says. "So I wanted to prove to everybody that small things do matter."

The Man of Steel stands atop the head of a pin.

See It in Rome

When is a city not a city? When it's VATICAN CITY—the smallest sovereign, or independent, country in the world. Some call it the Holy See, which means that it encloses the see, or area, ruled by the Pope—the leader of the Roman Catholic Church.

The area of Vatican City is 0.17 square mile (0.44 sq km)—slightly bigger than the National Mall in Washington, D.C.

Awesome Facts

● Vatican City is the home of the "mother" church of more than one billion Roman Catholics around the globe. It is a separate nation surrounded by Rome, the capital city of Italy.

● Fewer than 1,000 people live in Vatican City. The official languages are Italian and Latin, the language of ancient Rome and of traditional Catholic prayers.

● The Vatican's head of state is the Bishop of Rome, otherwise known as the Pope. "Pope" comes from the Greek word for "father." When one pope dies, his successor is elected in a secret meeting of Roman Catholic cardinals.

TOP 5
Five Smallest Countries in the World

COUNTRY	LOCATION	SIZE	POPULATION ESTIMATE
1. Vatican City	Italy	0.17 sq mi (0.44 sq km)	826
2. Monaco	Mediterranean Coast	0.75 sq mi (1.95 sq km)	32,965
3. Nauru	Western Pacific	8.11 sq mi (21 sq km)	14,019
4. Tuvalu	South Pacific	10 sq mi (26 sq km)	12,373
5. San Marino	Italy	24 sq mi (61 sq km)	30,324

Source: 2010 TFK Almanac

St. Peter's Basilica is the most famous landmark in Vatican City. It took more than 100 years to build the church which was begun in 1506. Many people think St. Peter's is the greatest building of the 16th century.

The enormous interior of St. Peter's, which can hold up to 60,000 people, is decorated with works by some of the world's greatest artists, including Michelangelo, Botticelli, and Bernini.

The Biggest Little Show on Earth

Come one, come all! The **HOWARD BROTHERS CIRCUS** is in town! It's the largest miniature circus in the world—and a childhood dream come true! The circus is on display at the John and Mable Ringling Museum of Art in Sarasota, Florida.

INCHES 1

Actual Size

LOU JACOBS

Awesome Facts

● The Howard Brothers Circus is named for **Howard Tibbals**, a circus lover since he was three years old.

● Based on Tibbals' huge collection of old circus photographs, the model recreates the Ringling Bros. and Barnum & Bailey Circus as it looked from 1919-38.

This photo shows one of eight tents that are featured in the circus. →

Tibbals worked for more than 50 years to make nearly 1,000,000 circus pieces by hand, at a scale of ³/₄ inch to the foot (1.9 cm).

Go ahead, count 'em: eight main tents, 1,300 circus performers and workers, 152 wagons, 7,000 folding chairs for customers, a 57-car train, more than 800 circus animals, and much, much more!

The model's perimeter is about 450 feet (137 m)— the length of 1.5 football fields!

Chapter 2

Awesome Price Tags

What does it cost to take a roundtrip voyage to the International Space Station or to buy a special doghouse? These are two of the items in this chapter that are for sale. Are they worth the awesome pricetags? You decide if the price is right or out of sight.

In This Chapter

- Costly Dogs
- Costlier Doghouses
- High-priced Baseball Cards
- And Much More...

For the Record

One of the first regularly-minted U.S. pennies is now worth a small fortune.

$$$$,$$$

A visit to the International Space Station is possible but only for a fortunate few.

$$\$\$\$,\$\$\$,\$\$\$$$

For the **Record**

The Dogue de Bordeaux (dog duh bore-*doh*), or French Mastiff, is one of the priciest canines to be found in any kennel.

$$\$\$,\$\$\$$$

Far-Out Prices

A penny, a doll, a doghouse, a puppy.
How much could those items add up to?

A Penny for Your Thoughts

Next time you spot a **penny** in the street, pick it up!
It might just be worth a fortune. This **1793 Sheldon NC-1
Chain cent** was one of the first regularly minted coins in the
United States. To find one of these rare coins, you'll need
plenty of luck: collectors believe that only four exist today.

$275,000

Rich Barbie

You can buy a Barbie for **$20** or less. But not this
jewel-studded doll, created in Mexico City to promote
a DVD, "Barbie and the Diamond Castle."
The cost accounts for the 318 diamonds sewn on her
gown and accessories. Wow. For that much, you
could buy **4,000 Barbies**, and lots of outfits
to fill her closets!

$94,800

Here's the perfect pad for a pricey pooch: a custom-made doghouse with running water, electricity, heat, and air conditioning. Before that pup moves in, though, better make sure it's house trained!

$30,000

How Much Is That Doggie?

The **FRENCH MASTIFF** is one high-priced puppy! Since the Middle Ages, this handsome breed has been reared to be hunters, fighters, and protectors. It may be true that money can't buy love, but French Mastiffs are said to be very loyal to their owners!

$8,670

TOP 5
Pricey Puppies

1. French Mastiff..........................$2,300 – $8,670
2. English Bulldog.......................$2000 – $5,000
3. Cavalier King Charles Spaniel.. $800 – $3500
4. Norfolk Terrier ....$2,000 – $3,000
5. Akita Inu.................................$1,500 – $3,500

Worth the Money?

Some prices are in the ballpark—while others are out of this world!

Costly Card

Speaking of baseball: **HONUS WAGNER**–nicknamed the Flying Dutchman—was a National League player from 1897-1917. Wagner was the shortstop for the Pittsburgh Pirates and one of the superstars of the great American sport. Trading cards with his picture, which were tucked into cigarette packets, are almost impossible to find. So one collector was willing to fork over a fortune for a piece of baseball history!

$1,265,000

Awesome Fact

About **$10** will buy you a 2009 set of baseball cards picturing today's baseball superstars, from the Yankees to the Phillies.

$777

Blue-Ribbon Burger

A Las Vegas reataurant has created a very high-priced hamburger. For **$777** customers can bite into a juicy patty made of Kobe beef—a flavorful meat from a certain breed of Japanese cattle—topped with chunks of lobster, caramelized onions, and lots of extras.

Trip to the Stars

For a one-of-a-kind vacation, an earthling can visit outer space! In 2007, an American billionaire paid **millions** to the Russians to train him to fly into space. His reward for the fee: a round-trip ticket to the International Space Station (ISS). His fellow passengers on the way home were an American astronaut and a Russian cosmonaut who had spent seven months working on the ISS.

$25,000,000

Book Your Flight Now

For $200,000, you can take a seat on a spacecraft owned by Richard Branson, a British billionaire with big ideas. His new company, Virgin Galactic, will fly passengers to a point almost 10 miles (16 km) above Earth. Then the airship will make a short, sub-orbital flight and passengers will be able to float around the cabin for about six minutes! Each trip will last about two-and-a-half hours.

That comes to **$1,333.33** per minute. So far, at least 300 people have signed up for the trip.

$200,000

N328KF

Chapter 3
AWESOME
Animals & Plants

In a far-off galaxy a planet teems with living creatures. Possible? Maybe. But for now, we know of only one place with the right conditions for life: Earth. Scientists say there are between 3 and 30 million species thriving on land, in the air, and under water. Each form of life on Earth is awesome in its own way, but some really stand out from the pack.

In This Chapter

For the Record

The **CHEETAH** is the fastest land animal—more than three times faster than the fastest human.

Awesome Fact

BAMBOO is the fastest-growing plant —and one of the most useful to humans.

Actual Size

Awesome Fact

Measuring over 6 inches (15 cm) long, the **TITAN BEETLE** is one of the biggest insects in the world.

For the Record

Not only is the **BLUE WHALE** the largest creature to live in the ocean—it is the largest mammal on Earth.

Dinosaurs Updated

DINOSAURS lived on Earth for 165 millions years and disappeared about 65 million years ago. Paleontologists—scientists who study dinosaurs—still hunt for the tracks and bones the animals left behind. That's because each discovery gives us new information about these awesome reptiles.

From TIME FOR KIDS Magazine

Now in Living Color!

U ntil now, most people thought dinosaurs were dull brown or grey. But were those its true colors? A team of paleontologists led by Michael Benton recently studied the fossils of *Sinosauropteryx* (sine-oh-sore-*op*-ter-iks), a meat-eater that lived 125 million years ago. These fossils, found in China, had traces of feathers, proving that dinosaurs and birds are somehow related.

Just looking at its feather-covered tail, Benton and his team could see stripes of white and some other hue that had faded over time. Then they looked at the feathers through a powerful microscope. Inside they saw tiny capsules called melanosomes (mel-*lan*-uh-sohmz).

Melanosomes contain a pigment, or coloring substance, that gives feathers, fur, or hair their color. Differently shaped melanosomes correspond to different colors. Melanosomes with a sausage shape produce dark brown. Ball-shaped melanosomes make orange. "We found only the ball type," reported Benton, "so, we knew that the feathers were orange!"

With the mystery of *Sinosauropteryx* now solved, Benton is eager to find out the colors of other dinosaurs. "We'll map out the colors over a whole dinosaur," he predicts, "so we can say "It had black splotches and green bits and stripes..." Dinosaur-lovers can hardly wait to see what colors come next!

An artist's view of *Sinosauropteryx* in color

Tiny Diny

A tiny fossil discovered in Colorado has been identified as **the smallest dinosaur in all North America**. The fast-running *Fruitadens* was only 28 inches (70 cm) long and weighed less than two pounds (0.9 kg).

INCHES 1

Actual Size

Woolly Baby

Distant cousins of the elephant, **woolly mammoths** died out 10,000 years ago. But in 2007, a reindeer herder hiking in frozen Siberia discovered a baby mammoth, perfectly preserved in the snow! Some scientists think that eventually they may be able to use the baby's DNA to bring a new woolly mammoth to life!

Life on the Galápagos

Take a boat to the **GALÁPAGOS** (gah-*la*-pa-goes) and see some of Earth's most amazing creatures up close. Just off the coast of Ecuador, in South America, these 19 volcanic islands in the Pacific Ocean are home to animals that have long been isolated from most predators and humans. Because of this, they are unusually tame. When the great scientist, Charles Darwin, paid a visit there in 1835, he got to thinking about how different species evolve, or change, over time. Today, a visitor can still see what Darwin saw: iguanas, sea lions, frigate birds, penguins, giant tortoises, sea turtles, and the comical blue-footed boobies.

● Marine iguanas of the Galápagos are the only lizards that can live in the ocean.

● Despite their fierce look, they are vegetarians that feed on seaweed.

Awesome Fact

The insect group with the greatest number of species—350,000 in all—is the beetle. There are **over 400** species of beetles in the Galápagos.

MEXICO
Mexico City
Gulf of Mexico
Tampa
Orlando
Miami
CUBA
Caribbean Sea
COLOMBIA
Bogota
Cali
GALAPAGOS ISLANDS
ECUADOR
Quito
Guayaquil
PERU

● Blue-footed boobies do a special dance to attract a mate. The male shows off his colorful feet and waves his wings to attract attention.

● Boobies are very skilled at diving for fish.

● About 50,000 sea lions frolic on the islands.

● They are not shy about playing with tourists in the surf.

● The Galápagos giant tortoise weighs up to 500 pounds (225 kg).

● The largest tortoise on earth, it can live over a hundred years.

Clever Birds

Calling somebody a "birdbrain" may be a compliment. Turns out **BIRDS** are a lot smarter and tougher than we thought. Today, biologists are seriously studying "avian intelligence"—that is, how some birds show a clever mind at work, whether hunting for food or finding their way back home.

Polly Wants a Dictionary

Watch what you say around an **African grey**! These super-smart parrots can learn hundreds of human words—and use them in just the right situation.

Excuse me . . .

Do you happen to have a cracker?

Awesome Fact

One of the most famous African grey parrots, named **Alex**, belonged to Irene Pepperberg ,an animal psychologist. Alex could say 150 words and name different objects, colors, and shapes. After working with Alex for 30 years, Pepperberg claimed that the bird had the intelligence of a five-year-old child.

Clark's Nutcracker

Can't remember where you put your cell phone? Think about **Clark's nutcrackers**. They hide their food in thousands of places … and can recall exactly where they buried each tidbit up to nine months later!

Helpful Hornbills

Hornbills can be very thoughtful of others! In Africa, one species of hornbill helps dwarf mongooses—small, meat-eating rodents— find food.

Awesome Fact

Hornbills can live up to 47 years.

Blast from the Past

Since the time of the ancient Egyptians, people have trained homing pigeons to carry secret messages back and forth. One French pigeon was given a medal for delivering 12 important messages during World War I (1914-1918).

Crows at Work

Picking up a tool to get something done is a sure sign of intelligence. In the past, scientists thought humans were the only tool-users on the planet. But now they know lots of animals use tools, including some birds. **New Caledonian crows** are often seen holding sticks in their beaks to pull insects out of logs.

Mind-Boggling Bugs

Experts say that insects on Earth today total **10 QUINTILLION** (that's a 10 plus 18 zeroes!). Since there are only 7 billion humans, we're way outnumbered! But we count on insects to keep the world buzzing: pollinating our plants, enriching the soil, even eating the bugs that really, really bug us!

For the Record

The dragonfly is the speed champion of the insect world. Its four long wings help it reach speeds of 50 to 60 miles (80-96 km) per hour.

Bugs of Steel

The **titan beetle** is one of the largest and strongest insects in the world. Adults can grow up to **6.5 inches (16.25 cm) long**. Their powerful mandibles, or jaws, can snap a pencil in two. Most adult titan beetles spend their time flying around looking for mates in their native habitat, the Amazon rainforest. That's where you can hear these titanic critters hissing at any enemy brave enough to attack them.

INCHES!

Actual Size

Killer Instinct

He may be small, but he's downright deadly! The **assassin bug** squirts toxic saliva into its victims and then sucks them dry. The good news is: some species of assassins have a taste for cockroaches and bedbugs!

What a Honey!

We're so used to seeing **honeybees** that we may forget how awesome they truly are. They manufacture a delicious food enjoyed by bears, people, and other bees. They make beeswax, honeycombs, and royal jelly. Bees communicate with each other, build elaborate hives, and pollinate billions of dollars of crops each year. Admire them —but stay clear of those stingers!

Bzzzzzzzzzz!!!!

P.U.!!!!

Foul Play

These guys could use a deodorant! Whenever they feel threatened, they release a foul-smelling liquid from the glands in their thorax—the part between the head and abdomen. No wonder they're called **stink bugs**!

Strange Sea Creatures

Marine biologists—scientists who study animals and plants that inhabit the sea—keep track of unique species that add to our understanding of life in the deep. They know that beneath the waves are schools of fantastic creatures you're not likely to see in an aquarium.

Batteries Not Included

The sun's rays don't reach the deepest parts of the ocean. Thank goodness for **flashlight fish**—bioluminescent fish that light up the dark waters. Their glowing "headlamps" are right beneath their eyes and shine a spotlight on tasty crabs or other edible shellfish floating by.

Awesome Fact

All the fish that are bioluminescent send out light that other fish can see in the dark. The light frightens predators and helps fish of the same species recognize each other.

Gulping Down Dinner

By opening wide its huge jaws—11 times the volume of its whole body—the **gulper eel** can swallow a fish as large as itself. If a school of shrimp happens by, that big mouth gulps them down by the hundreds!

The Ocean Layers

Scientists divide the ocean into five main layers, or zones. The first zone begins at the surface, where sunlight warms the water; the last zone begins some 36,100 feet (11,000 m) below in pitch-black areas where the water temperature is just above freezing. Amazingly, sea life exists in even the deepest zones!

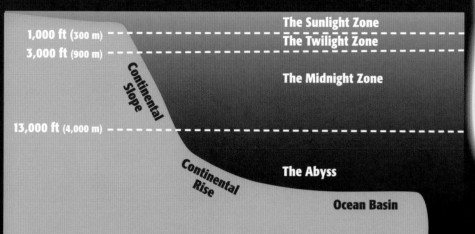

The Sunlight Zone
1,000 ft (300 m)
The Twilight Zone
3,000 ft (900 m)
The Midnight Zone
Continental Slope
13,000 ft (4,000 m)
Continental Rise
The Abyss
Ocean Basin
The Trenches
36,000 ft (11,000 m)

From TIME FOR KIDS Magazine

What a *berry* exciting find! In early 2010, scientists in Taiwan announced that they had discovered a new species of crab off the island nation's southern coast. With a bright red shell and tiny white spots, the little crustacean looks just like a ripe strawberry.

Awesome Fact

Camouflage helps sea creatures keep a low profile until they're ready to attack their prey. It also hides them from their own enemies.

Now You See It, Now You Don't

Frogfish can look like a coral reef or a stone on the sea floor. They can change color to blend in with their habitat. As a rule, these masters of disguise don't get around much; they prefer to lie in wait for fish or shellfish to happen by, unaware. Then the frogfish open wide—and suck in their meal with a rush of water.

Nocturnal Creatures

People who like to stay up late are called "night owls," a nickname based on **NOCTURNAL** birds hat sleep all day and hunt after dark. Many creatures of the night have fur or feathers that blend into the background—a camouflage that keeps them hidden from their enemies or their prey.

Giraffe of the Forest

A giraffe-like mammal from Congo in Africa, the **okapi** (oh-*kah*-pee) spends its nights chewing on plants, fruit, and berries. Its chocolate-brown coat and striped legs blend into the dense foliage of the jungles and forests where it finds food.

Whoo's There?

Owls are famous for their night-time prowls. But what do they do during the day? They sleep. Most owls have feathers that match the bark of the trees they nest in. This camouflage protects them from predators while they snooze.

Armed and Dangerous

If an **octopus** doesn't want to be seen, it simply changes its skin color to match its habitat. It can also squirt black ink into the water—the better to escape an enemy. Mostly a night-hunter, the octopus uses one of its eight arms to catch small fish, crabs, and other sea life—and then kills them by injecting poison into their bodies.

Spots in the Snow

When the sun goes down, the **snow leopard** goes into action, hunting wild sheep, birds, and other animals. These large and endangered cats live in the icy mountains of central Asia. Their grey or tan fur makes them hard to see against snow-covered rocks. Their keen eyesight and hearing enables them to hunt at night.

Spotted Lightning

CHEETAHS, the fastest land animals, can easily outpace the fastest humans. The record-breaking Usain Bolt ran the 100-meter dash (about 300 feet) in under ten seconds. If Bolt could keep going at that speed, he could run a mile in less than three minutes—a rate of 20 miles (32 km) per hour. But how does he measure up to the cheetah and other speedy land animals?

Clocked at 70 miles (112 km) per hour, or more than a mile a minute, the cheetah would easily win the gold in an Olympic sprint.

The cheetah's claws are semi-retractable—they pull into its paws part-way. When the animal runs, the claws act like cleats, providing extra grip on the ground.

A slim, lightweight body helps the cheetah reach 40 mph (64 kmph) in seconds.

TOP 5
Fastest Land Animals

ANIMAL, HABITAT

① Cheetah, Africa

② Pronghorn antelope, North America

③ Wildebeest, Africa

④ Lion, Africa

⑤ Thomson's gazelle, Africa

0   10 (16)   20 (32)   30 (48)   40 (64)   50 (80)   60 (96)   70 (112)

MILES (KM) PER HOUR

That long tail helps the cheetah stay
balanced when it's running at top speed.

Pronghorn antelope: It can easily outrun hungry enemies.

Wildebeest: Looks are deceiving: this animal can really move.

Lion: He's not the King of Athletes, but he is still a contender.

Thomson's gazelle: The cheetah is faster—but a gazelle has more staying power.

Honorable Mention

Even on four sturdy legs, the giant tortoise
would need five hours to go **one mile**
(1.6 km)—a rate of 1/5th of a mile per hour!

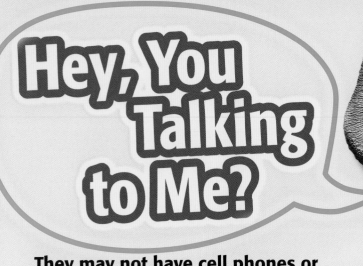

Hey, You Talking to Me?

They may not have cell phones or chat rooms, but animals constantly **COMMUNICATE** with each other. When you're out in nature, if you keep very still, you might just catch the buzz.

No, I'm talking to her!

Big Talk

Elephants make many sounds ranging from trumpet calls to deep rumbles. Each sound has a different meaning—from "Let's go!" to "I'm close by." Researchers are putting together an "elephant dictionary" that will help humans hear the difference between "Hello there!" and "Get out of my way!"

Let's go!

Bark!

Prairie Dog Parlance

The barks, squeals, and squeaks of **Gunnison prairie dogs**—members of the squirrel family who live in the American Southwest—may communicate detailed information about dangerous and hungry animals nearby. A short bark might actually mean: "Listen up everybody! There's a tall thin coyote nearby."

You sure?

Colorful Speech

Caribbean reef squid don't communicate with words—instead, they use color! These smart mollusks send messages to each other by changing the colors and patterns on their torpedo-shaped bodies.

**Ooh-Whee!!
Ooh-Whee!!**

Whistling in Dolphinese

Dolphins communicate through whistles-making hundreds of different signals that marine biologists are trying to understand. These small, friendly whales have distinct "voices," just like we do. Even a baby dolphin, or calf, learns to recognize its mother's call.

Meeting & Mating

When they're ready to reproduce, animals and insects have a range of mating habits. Some of these behaviors may look strange to humans—but they're all perfectly natural in the animal kingdom.

Galápagos Valentine

To attract attention during breeding season, male **frigate birds**, common to the Galápagos Islands, puff up their throat into a red, heart-shaped "valentine." That's the male's way of letting females know he's looking for a mate.

Dangerous Attraction

A male **praying mantis** is flirting with danger when he goes after a female praying mantis. After they mate, she may attack and eat him! Most of the time, though, her partner manages to escape.

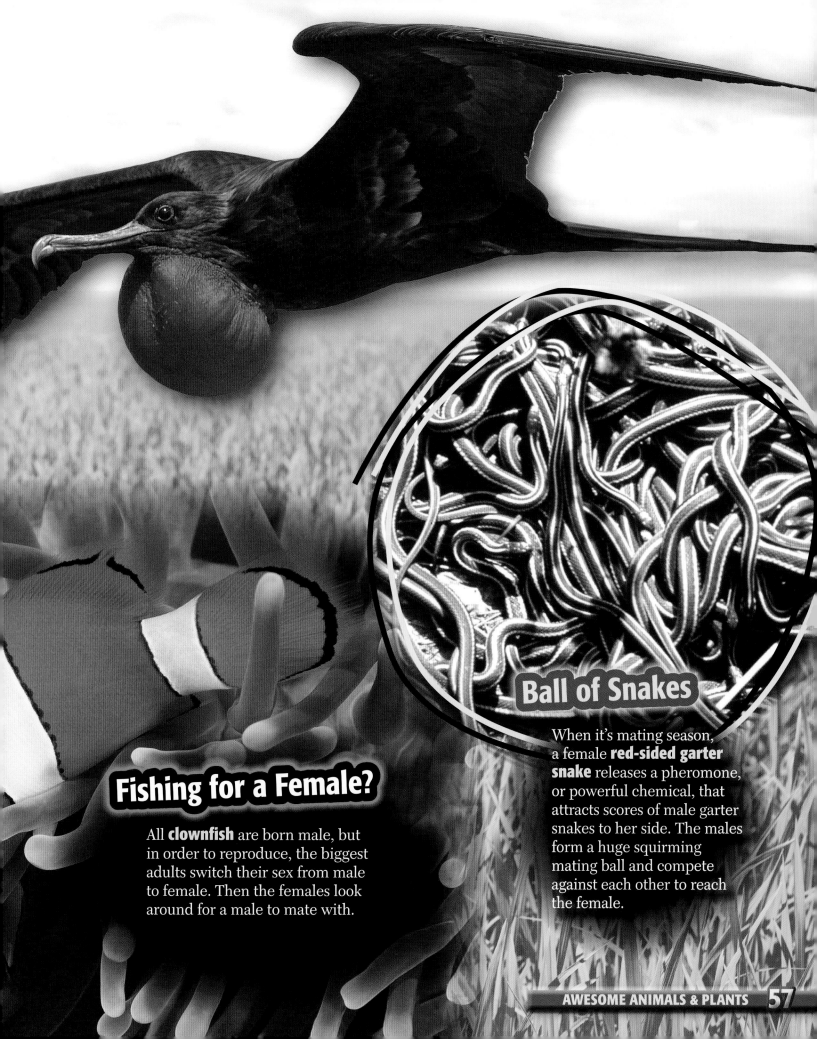

Fishing for a Female?

All **clownfish** are born male, but in order to reproduce, the biggest adults switch their sex from male to female. Then the females look around for a male to mate with.

Ball of Snakes

When it's mating season, a female **red-sided garter snake** releases a pheromone, or powerful chemical, that attracts scores of male garter snakes to her side. The males form a huge squirming mating ball and compete against each other to reach the female.

Animal First Responders

Firefighters pull pet cats, dogs, hamsters, snakes, and even ferrets from burning buildings. Beachcombers help stranded whales swim back out to sea. Bird-lovers return fallen chicks to their nests. But once in a while, **animals come to the rescue of humans—and sometimes of other animals!**

Who You Gonna Call?

When Kevin Weaver collapsed on the floor, his 3-year-old **beagle,** Belle, knew just what to do. She used her mouth to press down on the number 9 on Kevin's cell phone, connecting it to 911. Then she started barking—loud enough to convince the 911 operator that the caller was in trouble. Kevin, a diabetic, had trained Belle to press that number in case of an emergency—and she did— saving his life!

A Dog's Best Friend

You've heard of a seeing-eye dog–but how about a seeing-eye cat? What's more, a seeing-eye cat that helps a dog? In Pennsylvania, a 10-year-old **red tabby** named Libby took it upon herself to help Cashew, the 14-year-old family Labrador, who's blind and deaf, get through his doggy day. She leads him to his food and guides him safely around the house. There's nothing catty about that!

Parrot Sitter

MAMA!

A two-year-old girl was choking on a piece of Pop Tart—while her babysitter had gone to the bathroom. Luckily, the family's sharp-eyed **Quaker parrot** Willie was watching. He started screeching "Mama! Baby!" over and over until the sitter rushed back to see what was wrong—and to help the little girl cough up the food.

BABY!

Preserving Plants

The **EDEN PROJECT** in England collects and grows plants from around the world in dome-like biomes where temperature and moisture levels can be carefully controlled. Mindful that global climate change threatens habitats around the globe, the project directors want to preserve the wide variety of plant life that surrounds us and keeps our ecosystems in balance.

Awesome Fact

The Rainforest Biome in England is big enough to hold a stand of giant bamboo, one of the fastest-growing plants on Earth! Some species of bamboo can grow up to 24 inches (60 cm) or more each day, and can reach a height of 40-100 feet (12-31 m).

Awesome Fact

The word **biome** describes areas on Earth with similar climates, plants and animals.

Within a biome are smaller areas called habitats, where certain kinds of plant life can be found. For example, particular species of vines and orchids thrive in tropical rain forests; cactus and aloe plants grow in desert habitats.

Awesome Fact

On the surface of the earth, scientists have identified six major biomes: tropical rain forests, temperate forests, deserts, grasslands, taiga (areas with snowy winters and short wet summers), and tundra (cold, dry areas with windy winters and short summers).

Helpful Plants

Take a close look at the plants around you. Some day, you might need one to save your life! Ever since the Stone Age, humans have been learning the secrets of thousands of plants and using them to make powerful medicines.

Native American tribes have long made tea from the bark of the white willow to soothe aches and pains.

Water in a Barrel

Stranded in the desert? Are you hungry and thirsty? Go find a **barrel cactus**. You can squeeze out the water it stores in its pulp. You can even roast the cactus over a campfire. Just be careful of those spines.

Awesome Fact

Many stores selling juice drinks blend the fruit of the **barrel cactus** into smoothies.

The largest cactus in the American Southwest, the barrel cactus can live up to 130 years old!

The Wonderful Willow

In the ancient world, healers discovered that the leaves and bark of the **willow tree** could be used to treat headaches, body pains, and fever. In 1828, a German scientist removed the chemical in willow bark that relieves pain. He called it *salix*, the Latin word for willow tree. Today, a form of that chemical is a key ingredient in aspirin.

The veins in all leaves are like pipes that circulate water and nutrients throughout the plant.

Healing Aloe Vera

The juicy **aloe vera plant** (al-oh *veer*-ah) is nature's first-aid kit. Green, gooey gel made from its leaves soothes burns and sunburns and helps to cure cuts and wounds.

Aloe vera gel is inside the leaf of the plant. When the skin of the leaf is peeled off on one side, the gel can be scooped out with a spoon.

Aloe Vera is a succulent, or water-saving, plant. Although it thrives in dry areas, it has shallow roots that absorb the dew or droplets from a light rain shower.

For the Record

Almost 25% of the medicines sold in drug stores are made directly from plants. But as global warming heats up our planet, the higher temperatures may make some life-saving plants disappear.

What's for Dinner?

Most plants live on sunlight, water, carbon dioxide, and minerals in the soil. But a few are **CARNIVORES** —that means, they prefer a diet of fresh "meat." They lure living insects to their doom!

YUM!!

Fly Catcher

The star of insect-eating plants is the **Venus fly trap** a native of the southwestern United States. Named after the Roman goddess of love, it opens its leaves to welcome a passing bug. Then, snap! Dinnertime!

Awesome Fact

Sometimes carnivorous plants trap and eat small frogs and mammals.

A Pitcher of Danger

Lurking in swamps and bogs is the deadly **pitcher plant**. When it blooms, out comes a beautiful, pitcher-shaped flower whose nectar attracts hungry insects. But once a bug lands, it slides down a slippery slope—and drowns in a pool of water deep inside the flower.

Awesome Facts

● Carnivorous plants are usually found in areas where the soil lacks minerals and other nutrients. The plants need nutritious bugs to survive!

● Meat-eating plants, which can grow up to 10 feet (3 m) tall, are found everywhere in the world—except Antarctica.

Sneaky Sundew

Sundew ... such a pretty name, and such a double-crossing plant. Mosquitoes, gnats, and other small insects can't resist the sticky nectar on its leaves. When the bugs land on the plant to feed they get stuck. While they struggle to get free, the sundew squirts them with digestive juices that turn the bugs into a meal.

Bountiful Bamboo

BAMBOO, the largest member of the grass family, is one amazing plant. Different species of bamboo are found on almost every continent. It's renewable—that is, quick and easy to grow; it doesn't need pesticides that harm the soil; and its many uses save us from cutting down other types of trees. But don't plant it in your backyard—it's so fast-growing, it can easily crowd out other plants nearby.

Awesome Fact

Unlike plastic and other artificial building materials, bamboo is 100% biodegradable. It can be broken down by other living creatures and safely recycled into the environment.

For the Record

Bamboo is the fastest-growing plant on Earth! It can shoot up to its full height in four months or less! Some species can grow up to 24 inches (60 cm) or more each day, and can reach a height of 40-100 feet (12-31 m).

Awesome Bamboo

Check out all the things you can do with bamboo:

- Set the table with bamboo placemats.

- Cut up carrots on a bamboo cutting board.

- Eat tender bamboo shoots from a bamboo bowl.

- Brush your teeth over a bamboo sink.

- Dance on a bamboo floor.

- Fence in your yard with bamboo.

- Stretch out in a bamboo chair to read a book.

- Wear a T-shirt made of bamboo threads.

- Play a tune on a bamboo flute.

Awesome Fact

Giant pandas in China eat various types of bamboo for breakfast, lunch, and dinner: 20-40 pounds (9-18 kg) of shoots, stems, and leaves each day! But as more and more humans clear land for their own use, pandas are in danger of losing their food supply.

Chapter 4
Awesome Sports

SPORTS, GAMES, and CONTESTS have drawn enthusiastic crowds for thousands of years. Whether you're a player or a fan, whether you compete with muscle power or brain power, there are more exciting sports and competitions today than ever before, and more records to be set and broken!

For the Record

LANCE ARMSTRONG wins a record-breaking seven straight Tour de France bicycle races between 1999–2005.

In This Chapter

- Extreme Sports
- Perfect Scores
- Mind Games
- And Much More...

Terrific Snowboarding

A mix of surfing, skateboarding, and skiing, **SNOWBOARDING** has been popular for years, but it's a fairly new Olympic sport. American snowboarders earned most of the medals at the 2010 Winter Olympics in Vancouver, Canada.

AIRBORNE A daring snowboarder demonstrates the **540 McTwist**, spinning his board one-and-a-half rotations in mid-air.

A WOMAN'S STAR TURN

Snowboarders perform jumps, twists, backflips, and other hair-raising turns from inside a half-pipe, a huge bowl-shaped structure built out of snow. **Kelly Clark** was 19 years old when she won a gold medal for the women's half-pipe competition at the 2002 Winter Olympics.

SKY-HIGH FINCH Breaking speed and height records are important goals for competitors like Andy Finch.

SHOOTING STAR At the 2010 Winter Olympic Games in Vancouver, 23-year-old superstar Shaun White captured two gold medals for his mind-blowing runs in the half-pipe, plunging down a 550-foot chute of ice and racing skyward up 22-foot walls. People are still talking about White's spectacular finale, the Double McTwist 1260: three-and-a-half twists combined with two flips.

BIRD'S-EYE VIEW
One high-flying photographer shot Shaun White in action from above.

Great Upsets

It's great when the favorite team or player wins the game—but it can be even more thrilling when an underdog comes from behind and goes on to victory.

For the Record

Contestants in the tough Tour de France spend three weeks racing across 2,178 miles (3,505 km) of French countryside and steep mountain roads.

Bicycle Champions

America's Lance Armstrong is the only cyclist to win the Tour de France seven times in a row. Lance took a break from racing in 2005, and returned in the 2009 race. Alberto Contador of Spain took up the challenge in 2009, and made it first across the finish line. Armstrong came in third place after Andy Schleck, from Luxembourg.

Robin

For the Record

TENNIS TURNAROUND

Rafael Nadal was confident he would win the French Open in May, 2009. He was the four-time defending champion and the ranked Number One tennis player in the world. But he didn't count on the powerful forehand of a 24-year-old Swedish player, Robin Soderling, who had never gotten past the third round in a Grand Slam Competition. Soderling scored the biggest upset of the year, ending Nadal's 31-match winning streak in France.

Rafael

LACOST

For the Record

Top tennis players regualrly serve balls at more than 70 mph (113 kmph). The fastest serve ever recorded—163.6 mph (262.8 kmph)—was made by Bill Tilden in 1931. Venus Williams has delivered the fastest serve by a woman— 128 mph (205 kmph).

National Pastimes

ROOTING FOR THE HOME TEAM

People in different countries go crazy over different sports. Here are some that draw big crowds.

ALASKA
In the Iditarod, sled dogs and their musher, or trainer, race across frozen landscapes.

CUBA Baseball is the game in parts of South America and the Caribbean, especially Cuba.

BRAZIL An Afro-Brazilian martial art combined with music and dance, Capoeira (cap-oh-*way*-rah) is often performed on the streets.

RUSSIA
Rhythmic gymnasts perform coordinated routines that make Russian crowds cheer.

JAPAN Sumo, an ancient ritual practiced mostly in Japan, pits one giant wrestler against another.

INDIA
English-style cricket is popular in India and other countries that once belonged to the British Empire.

CHINA
Table tennis is a favorite sport—and players start training at a very young age.

TOP 5
World's Most Popular Team Sports

SPORT	WORLD CHAMPIONSHIPS	CHAMPIONSHIP SERIES
1. Soccer ("football"): World Cup		2010, 2014
2. Cricket: Cricket World Cup		2011, 2015
3. Basketball: FIBA World Championship		2010, 2014
4. Baseball: World Baseball Classic		2013, 2017
5. Rugby: World Cup		2011, 2015

Source: http: // www.worldsbiggest.com/2010/04/top-10-most-popular-team-sports-in.html

Perfect Timing

Nobody's perfect—but sometimes athletes make perfect moves to win a game or competition. And when they do, they're thrilling to see!

PERFECT PITCH In major league baseball, a **perfect game** means the pitcher throws so well that the opposing team never makes it to first base. Only 16 official perfect games have been pitched in major league baseball since 1900.

1956

DON LARSEN of the New York Yankees pitches a perfect game against the Brooklyn Dodgers in the fifth game of the World Series—the only perfect game in World Series history!

1999

DAVID CONE of the New York Yankees pitches a perfect game against the Montreal Expos with a total of only 88 pitches and 10 strike-outs. That's the fewest number of pitches in any perfect game since 1908.

2009

MARK BUEHRLE, a southpaw (left-hander), pitches a perfect game for the Chicago White Sox against the Tampa Bay Rays.

PERFECT DUNK People are still talking about Michael Jordan and the sixth game of the NBA championships in 1998. With only 5.2 seconds to spare, Jordan made a winning 20-foot shot that gave his team, the Chicago Bulls, a one-point win over the Utah Jazz—and the Bulls' sixth NBA championship.

SIMPLY PERFECT At the 1976 Summer Olympic Games in Montreal, Canada, 14-year-old **Nadia Comaneci** of Romania became the first gymnast in Olympic history to score a perfect 10. By the close of the games, she had earned six more perfect scores.

Taking Risks

For daredevil athletes, a great sport is a dangerous sport! While some people think that extreme sports are more like stunts than athletics, the athletes say that they are developing the skill of facing and conquering fear.

Walking on Ice

Packing ice axes, screws, and ropes, well-trained climbers are ready to work their way up a frozen waterfall or an ice-covered cliff. The Canadian Rockies are a favorite site for ice climbers to sharpen their skills.

Crazy Canoeing

Paddling gently down a stream just doesn't cut it for some folks. Athletes who love extreme water sports aren't satisfied unless they're taking their canoe or kayak down dangerous whitewater rapids, or even a steep waterfall.

For the Record

In January 2010, two experienced BASE jumpers, Omar Alhegelan and Nasser Al Neyadi, were given permission to leap from the top of Burj Khalifa, the tallest building in the world. After a 10-second free fall, they opened their parachutes and landed safely 2,205 feet (672 m) below, setting a new world record for the highest jump from a human-made structure.

Jumping from Home Base

BASE stands for buildings, antennas, spans (bridges), and Earth (cliffs)—all the places a fearless jumper (equipped with a parachute) can go to make a free-fall plunge. BASE jumping is more extreme than skydiving because athletes begin their jump at a low altitude which makes the plunge more dangerous. And they must land in a very small area, which takes a great deal of skill.

Mind Games

The ancient Greeks believed that people should have strong minds in strong bodies. In board games, word games, and other non-athletic competitions, people build up brain power in fun and challenging ways.

Your Move

Chess, "the game of kings," began in India and became a favorite pastime of noblemen in medieval Europe. Today, chess fans follow exciting international matches that pit top players, called grandmasters, against one another, and sometimes against a computer. World champion grandmaster Garry Kasparov outplayed a supercomputer, Deep Blue, in 1996, only to be defeated—by one game—in a 1997 rematch!

Awesome Fact

The title Grandmaster is awarded by the World Chess Federation to male and female players who have shown exceptional skill in official chess tournaments. While 9-year-old Hetul Shah defeated a grandmaster, he still has a way to go to earn the title himself.

TOP 5 Grandmasters Below Age 15

Name	Country	Age
1. Sergey Karjakin:	Ukraine	12 years, 7 months
2. Parimarjan Negi:	India	13 years, 4 months, 22 days
3. Magnus Carlsen:	Norway	13 years, 4 months, 27 days
4. Bu Xiangzhi:	China	13 years, 10 months, 13 days
5. Richard Rapport:	Hungary	13 years, 11 months, 6 days

Source: http://players.chessdom.com/jorge-cori

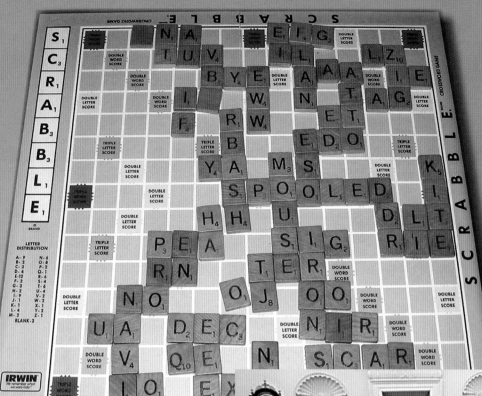

Seven Letter Words

Arrange your tiles and keep your eye on that triple word square! Serious Scrabble players can face off at the National Scrabble Championship, the largest Scrabble competition in the United States. To win this tournament, you don't need to learn definitions—but you do have to study the list of acceptable words compiled by the official Dictionary Committee!

Former President George W. Bush posing with Scripps National Spelling Bee winner, Sameer Mishra, in the Oval Office of the White House.

How Do You Spell Bzzzzz?

Spelling bees are great ways to learn new words. School Bees are also good practice for the Scripps National Spelling Bee, where kids 15 years old and younger can compete. The champion wins more than $40,000 in cash prizes, scholarships, and savings bonds.

For the Record

Winning Words from the Scripps National Spelling Bee

Year	Word	Pronunciation	Meaning
2009	Laodicean	lay-oh-dih-*see*-an	lukewarm, indifferent
2008	guerdon	*gur*-dn	reward
2007	serrefine	*sehr*-feen	small medical clamp
2006	ursprache	*oor*-shpra-kuh	imagined ancestor of a language
2005	appoggiatura	ah-pudge-ah-*tur*-ah	type of musical note

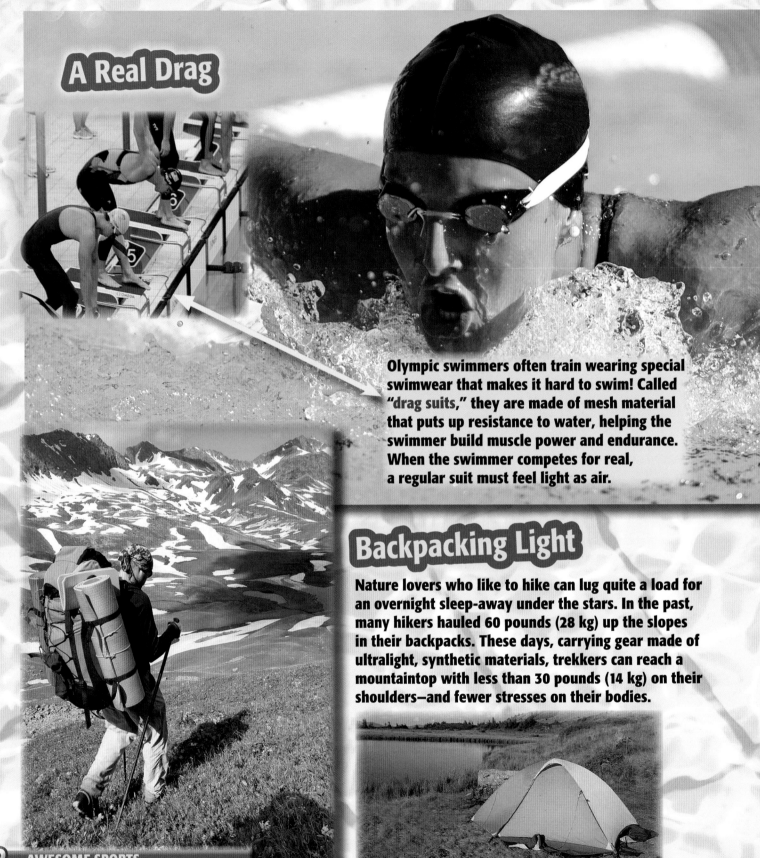

A-1 Gear

Sports gear designers study how competitive athletes play their game. The designers then come up with all kinds of equipment that helps make athletes better at their sport.

A Real Drag

Olympic swimmers often train wearing special swimwear that makes it hard to swim! Called "drag suits," they are made of mesh material that puts up resistance to water, helping the swimmer build muscle power and endurance. When the swimmer competes for real, a regular suit must feel light as air.

Backpacking Light

Nature lovers who like to hike can lug quite a load for an overnight sleep-away under the stars. In the past, many hikers hauled 60 pounds (28 kg) up the slopes in their backpacks. These days, carrying gear made of ultralight, synthetic materials, trekkers can reach a mountaintop with less than 30 pounds (14 kg) on their shoulders—and fewer stresses on their bodies.

Old diving
equipment

New lightweight
mouthpiece and gauge

Blast from the Past

In the past, scuba divers had to wear lots of clunky equipment— metal helmets, diving suits, shoes, tanks, and more—weighing up to 190 pounds (85.5 kg). Nowadays, scuba gear is much lighter— about 30-40 pounds (14-18 kg) on average—and more flexible, allowing divers to keep up easily with schools of beautiful fish!

Great Shoes

Paula Radcliffe, a world marathon record holder, uses high-tech running shoes to train. The shoe has a chip inside that transmits time, distance, speed, and calories burned to a mp3 player. Radcliffe and her trainers can study the information from the chip to help her run more efficiently.

Wild and Wacky Sports

People are always looking for new ways to get exercise and amuse themselves. Sometimes they dream up odd versions of traditional games. Sometimes they make up something silly and turn it into a tradition.

Down to Earth

The game of Quidditch is a bewitching sport played in the air by Harry Potter and friends at Hogwarts. But can it be played on land, without the ability to fly? Some young athletes think so. In their version of the game, they run around a field "riding" brooms while trying to throw volleyballs through six home-made hoops.

Going Toe to Toe

It will probably never be an Olympic event, but toe wrestling competitions in England are now drawing crowds and lots of feet. The idea is to lock big toes and push the opponent's foot to the ground. The rules don't say if toenail polish is allowed!

Hold Your Breath

As if chasing a hockey puck on land or ice weren't hard enough, now hockey-lovers push it around underwater. The new sport, called Octopush, was first played in England in 1954 and has spread to Australia, New Zealand, and South Africa.

Tube Be or Not Tube Be

In some cities you can start competing at five years old in an unusual sport organized by the Cardboard Tube Fighting League. As the league name suggests, it's a kind of sword fight, only instead of swords, the duelers use long cardboard tubes. The first one to break the other's tube wins.

Chapter 5
AWESOME
Eats

Forget the mac'n'cheese. The world is full of **AWESOME** foods to eat— and people who do amazing things with food. Some seek out the most unusual dishes to munch on. Others snarf down edibles in record time. Still others use food to make incredible constructions.

For the Record

Meet **JOEY CHESTNUT**, a champion hot dog eater

In This Chapter

- Insects on the Menu
- A Bird's Nest in the Soup
- Seed Spitting Contests
- And Much More...

The **DURIAN**, called "the king of fruits" in Southeast Asia, is probably the smelliest and sweetest fruit in the world.

Awesome Fact

Fried grasshoppers and other edible insects are a popular snack in many countries, including Mexico and Thailand.

Awesome Fact

Creative bakers turn gingerbread into prize winners.

The Unusual Food Club

The saying goes that "One man's meat is another man's poison." In other words, a dish that one person loves may make another person turn green. Here's a look at some foods that people either love or can't stomach!

Want Eel Soda with Your Sushi?

Served over rice or in a sushi roll, broiled unagi (ou-*na*-ghee), or eel, is a popular dish in Japan. Now the Japanese can wash it down with Unagi Nobori—a fizzy drink made out of eels and vitamins. Eel soda is just one of several unusual soft drinks enjoyed by the Japanese. A hot new flavor in Japan, Ice Cucumber, mixes cucumbers with cola!

Hold Your Nose!

The super-sweet **durian** is possibly the smelliest fruit on the planet—but that doesn't keep it from being a big favorite throughout Southeast Asia. Fans love the fruit's creamy, sugary insides and ignore the smell. Durian haters compare its odor and taste to moldy socks or rotting onions.

Fun Fact

In San Francisco, California, folks with a taste for insects have formed a club: B.A.B.E.S., the Bay Area Bug Eating Society. They hold bug cook-outs, share bug recipes, and post nutrition facts for many edible species!

Awesome Fact

In Singapore, an island nation in Southeast Asia, it is illegal to carry **durians** on buses and trains or to take them into hotels!

CRICKETS

Amount/Serving	%DV*	Amount/Serving	%DV*
Total Fat 5.5 g	11%	Total Carb. 0 g	0%
Sat Fat n/a g	n/a%	Fiber n/a g	n/a%
Cholest. n/a mg	n/a %	Sugars 0 g	n/a%
Sodium n/a mg	n/a%	Protein 6.7g	13%
Potassium n/a mg	n/a%		

Vitamin A n/a% - Vitamin C 0% - Calcium 9% - Iron 63%

TERMITES

Nutrition Facts

Serv. Size 100 g
Calories 613
Fat Cal. N/A

*Percent Daily Values(DV) are based on a 2,000 calorie diet.

Amount/Serving	%DV*	Amount/Serving	%DV*
Total Fat n/a g	n/a %	Total Carb.0 g	0%
Sat Fat n/a g	n/a %	Fiber n/a g	n/a %
Cholest. n/a mg	n/a %	Sugars 0 g	0%
Sodium n/a mg	n/a %	Protein 14.2g	28%
Potassium n/a mg	n/a %		

Vitamin A 0% - Vitamin C 0% - Calcium 5% - Iron n/a% (35.5mg)

CATERPILLARS

Nutrition Facts

Serv. Size 100 g
Calories 370
Fat Cal. 50.4

*Percent Daily Values(DV) are based on a 2,000 calorie diet.

Amount/Serving	%DV*	Amount/Serving	%DV*
Total Fat n/a g	n/a %	Total Carb. 0 g	0%
Sat Fat n/a g	n/a%	Fiber n/a g	n/a%
Cholest. n/a mg	n/a %	Sugars 0 g	0%
Sodium n/a mg	n/a%	Protein 28.2g	56%
Potassium n/a mg	n/a%		

Vitamin A 0% - Vitamin C 0% - Calcium n/a% - Iron n/a%

Saliva Soup

One of the most expensive items on Chinese menus is **Bird's Nest soup**. Its special ingredient is the saliva that birds called swifts use to make their nests. Workers usually collect the nests, which are high up in the walls of caves, before the birds have laid their eggs. After collecting two nests from each bird, the workers leave the swifts in peace to lay their eggs—and then remove the last nest once the babies have flown away.

swifts' nests

Awesome Fact

Bugs are loaded with protein but many are also loaded with calories. About 3.5 ounces (100 g) of crickets add up to 562 calories—about the same as a Big Mac.

Yum-o!

Daring diners don't mind a few bugs on their plate—in fact, they put them there. Insects have long been a part of people's diets and are still served in many parts of the world. In Mexico, fried grasshoppers are a common snack. In the South American nation of Colombia, people like to munch on roasted ants. And for a sweet treat you can't beat a chocolate-covered scorpion from China!

Fun with Food

At the dinner table, food fights are forbidden. But fighting for first prize at a famous food fest is fine.

Homes, Sweet Homes

At the **National Gingerbread House Competition** in Asheville, North Carolina, the treats are not for eating—just admiring. Every fall, contestants of all ages enter beautiful gingerbread houses in the hope of winning the grand prize. The judges' picks are put on display for the public to see—but not taste!

Food for Thoughtfulness

About 20 years ago, the Cypress Corporation, a high-tech company in California, thought up a great idea to support a local food bank. Through its yearly **Canned Food Sculpture contest**, different departments at the company compete to collect tons of canned and packaged foods. They use them to create amazing sculptures—such as a spaceship made of cans of peas and a Hummer made of cracker boxes! When the contest is over, every bit of food is given to needy families.

Independence Day is the perfect holiday for eating hot dogs—especially at Nathan's Famous hot dog stand in Coney Island, an amusement park in Brooklyn, New York. Every year, tens of thousands of people flock to Nathan's International July Fourth Hot Dog Eating Contest to watch contestants gobble the wieners with lightning speed.

Wolfing Down Dogs

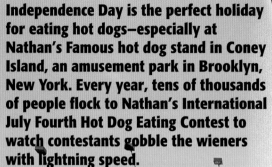

For The Record

As of 2009, Joey Chestnut holds Nathan's record for swallowing 68 hot dogs, buns and all, in 10 minutes. Chestnut enters all kinds of eating contests. Fortunately, most people can't stomach this kind of competition.

Spit and Win?

They love their watermelons in the small town of Luling, Texas! In the main event at an annual festival, the **Watermelon Thump**, people see how far they can spit two watermelon seeds. Champions can land the seeds up to 68 feet (21 m) away! The winner gets $500.

Chapter 6
Awesome Arts

People make masks from papier maché, build castles out of sand, and turn snow into snowmen. Some people make music from water glasses. Still other people get ideas for designing buildings from things they see in the world around them. There is an endless variety of materials hidden in plain sight that are just waiting to be transformed into works of art.

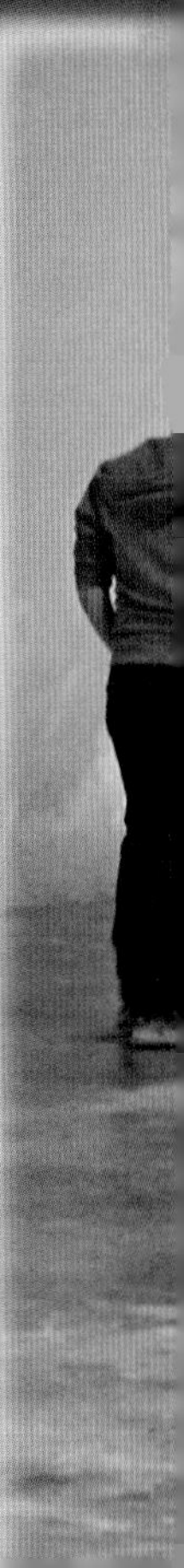

In This Chapter

- ○ LEGO® Brick Art
- ○ Watery Music
- ○ Astonishing Architecture
- ○ And Much More...

Awesome Fact

Wolfgang Amadeus Mozart, the great Austrian composer (1756-1791), wrote music for the glass harmonica—crystal goblets filled with water.

Awesome Fact

Frank Gehry, one of the world's leading architects, has created a building in Los Angeles that looks like a ship with all its sails up.

Awesome Fact

Sculptor John Chamberlain takes crushed sheet metal from old, wrecked cars and turns them into art. While his work can be seen in many museums, a big collection of Chamberlain's junk-car sculptures is on permanent display in an art center in Marfa, Texas.

Unusual Materials Make Unusual Art

An artwork starts with inspiration—a great idea. Then the artist finds the right materials to express that idea in a unique way.

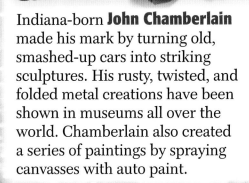

Car-tist

Indiana-born **John Chamberlain** made his mark by turning old, smashed-up cars into striking sculptures. His rusty, twisted, and folded metal creations have been shown in museums all over the world. Chamberlain also created a series of paintings by spraying canvasses with auto paint.

Playful Art

Sean Kenney loved playing with LEGO® bricks when he was a little boy. That playtime turned out to be the warm-up for an unusual career. Today, the New York-based artist uses LEGO® pieces to create amazing portraits and sculptures. His work ranges in size from small chairs and trucks to a giant model of Yankee Stadium made of more than 45,000 LEGO® pieces. He also made 30 life-size animals—from polar bears to penguins—for an exhibit at the Philadelphia Zoo.

Disappearing Art

Most artists hope their work will be admired in a museum. But not **Andy Goldsworthy**. This British artist creates many artworks in the great outdoors, where he uses the objects that nature provides—from stones and pebbles to leaves or even icicles. After he makes the work, he takes a photograph of it to sell or add to his portfolio. Then he walks away, leaving his creation to nature.

Goldsworthy's stone "egg" is called a cairn, an ancient form of sculpture found in the British Isles. Cairns may have been built to mark burial sites or places where ceremonies or rituals were held. The artist expects that in time, his cairn will be worn away by wind, water, and other natural forces.

Bold New Buildings

From traditional snow-block igloos to modern all-glass houses, buildings can be made from different and unusual materials. Twenty-first century architects use their imaginations to shape these materials into structures that grab people's attention.

Awesome Facts

• The Walt Disney Concert Hall in Los Angeles is named for the famous animator and creator of Disneyland. Canada-born architect Frank Gehry designed the building to resemble a ship with its sails waving in the wind.

• The curved, stainless steel walls of the Walt Disney Concert Hall make it look like a giant piece of sculpture.

• To design the building, Gehry started with a hand-drawn sketch. He and his team then created a model from clay, plastic, and other materials. Once the design was complete, Gehry's team used a computer program to make a 3-D computer model of the building.

Awesome Fact

People living nearby complained that the sun's reflection off the Walt Disney Concert Hall made their apartments too hot! Gehry's company fixed the problem by sanding down and dulling the reflective spots on the outside walls.

A Palace in Spain

Spanish architect Santiago Calatrava (kal-ah-*trah*-va) designed the **Queen Sophia Palace of the Arts** in Valencia, Spain, using a mix of steel, concrete, granite, glass, and ceramics. The building has three halls for different types of performances, conferences, and lectures. To some people, it looks like a spaceship; to others it resembles a giant helmet or an eye socket. What does it look like to you?

Awesome Fact

The Queen Sophia Palace of the Arts is named after Queen Sophia, the wife of Juan Carlos I of Spain. Juan Carlos I became king of Spain in 1975, and helped his country develop from a dictatorship into a democracy.

Musical Marvels

"Music is the art of thinking with sounds," a music professor once wrote. Here are three musical instruments that are simple to play, and whose sounds are simply beautiful.

Crystal-clear Sounds

Take a dozen crystal wine glasses, fill them with different amounts of water, and what do you get? A delightful musical instrument called the **GLASS HARMONICA** that has been around since the 18th century. Musicians stopped using glass harmonicas sometime in the 19th century because the instruments were hard to hear in a big concert hall. Glass harmonicas have made a comeback in recent years, and are sometimes included in symphony orchestras and rock bands.

Awesome Fact

Glass harmonicas are also known as crystallophones—meaning they produce sound from vibrating crystal, or glass. Rubbing your finger on the glass produces a wave of vibration, or resonant wave, that travels through the glass. The sound of the tone that each glass makes depends partly on the thickness of the glass and how much water is in it.

Awesome Fact

In 1762, the famous American inventor Benjamin Franklin redesigned the glass harmonica. He named his instrument "armonica," from the Italian word for harmony.

Bang on a Lid

Hanging pot tops from plumbing pipes is all it takes to make an **AQUAGGASWACK**, (ak-*wa*-gah-swack). It looks pretty wacky, but this home-made instrument produces bell-like tones when you tap on the lids with mallets, sticks, or brushes.

Awesome Fact

The first aquaggaswack was created by Curtis Settino, an American experimental musician and artist, in 1996.

Bang on Another Lid

The kettle gongs in the gamelan, a group of instruments that includes xylophones and drums, sound like the aquaggaswack. The gamelan is played throughout Indonesia, a chain of islands in Southeast Asia.

Chapter 7
Just Awesome

Why travel to the moon or Mars for spectacular scenery? From rain forests to mountain peaks, from canyons to desert dunes, Planet Earth has some of the most awesome sights to be seen in our galaxy.

In This Chapter

- Awesome Waterfalls
- Is It Earth or Is It Mars?
- Human-made Wonders of the World, Old and New
- And Much More...

Awesome Fact

The **GREAT PYRAMID** of Khufu in Egypt was one of the Great Wonders of the Ancient World—and it's still standing!

For the Record

ANGEL FALLS, in the South American country of Venezuela, is one of the tallest waterfalls discovered so far, with a dizzying drop of 2,647 feet (807 m). That's about half a mile!

Awesome Fact

This could be a desert on **EARTH** or a landscape on **MARS**. Pick your planet—and turn to page 102 to find the answer.

Wish You Were... Where?

For centuries, earthlings have been fascinated with exploring outer space, especially our closest neighbor—**MARS**. New and powerful telescopes and high-tech spacecraft help us get sharp photographs of other planets in our solar system. But do we really have to land on Mars to get an idea of what it looks like? There are parts of Planet Earth that look almost the same!

Which of the "postcards" shows a place on Earth? Which shows a landscape on Mars? Match each postcard with the captions below. (Answers are upside down.)

1 Ice-filled Crater on Mars
Scientists were thrilled to see water on Mars—in a crater filled with ice near the Martian North Pole.

2 Meteor Crater (Arizona)
A giant meteor crater slammed into the Earth 40,000 years ago, leaving its mark on what is now the U.S. state of Arizona. The crater is 3/4 of a mile (1.186 km) in diameter and 570 feet (170 m) deep.

3 Gobi Desert
Trekkers in the Gobi Desert, in China and Mongolia, might think they're on Mars—until they see plant life peeking from the sandy soil.

4 Surface of Mars
The *Mariner* spacecraft took this photo of the surface of Mars. See why it's called "the red planet"?

Answers: 1.d, 2.c, 3.a, 4.b

An Ancient Wonder, Still Standing

In 450 B.C., a Greek historian, Herodotus, came up with the idea of listing the most wondrous things in the world to see. Herodotus named seven great man-made marvels that awed the tourists of his time. Only one is left standing—the Great Pyramid of Khufu in Egypt—and it's still a must-see, more than 4,000 years after it was built.

The Great Pyramid of Khufu was constructed during the reign of King Khufu (also known as Cheops), ruler of Egypt from around 2589 B.C. to 2566 B.C.

The Seven Ancient Wonders of the World

STRUCTURE	LOCATION
1. The Great Pyramid of Khufu	Egypt
2. The Hanging Gardens of Babylon	Iraq
3. The Colossus of Rhodes	Greece
4. The Statue of Zeus at Olympia	Greece
5. The Mausoleum at Halicarnassus	Turkey
6. The Temple of Artemis at Ephesus	Turkey
7. The Lighthouse of Alexandria	Egypt

The 2,300,000 stone blocks used to build the pyramid weighed about 2.5 tons each!

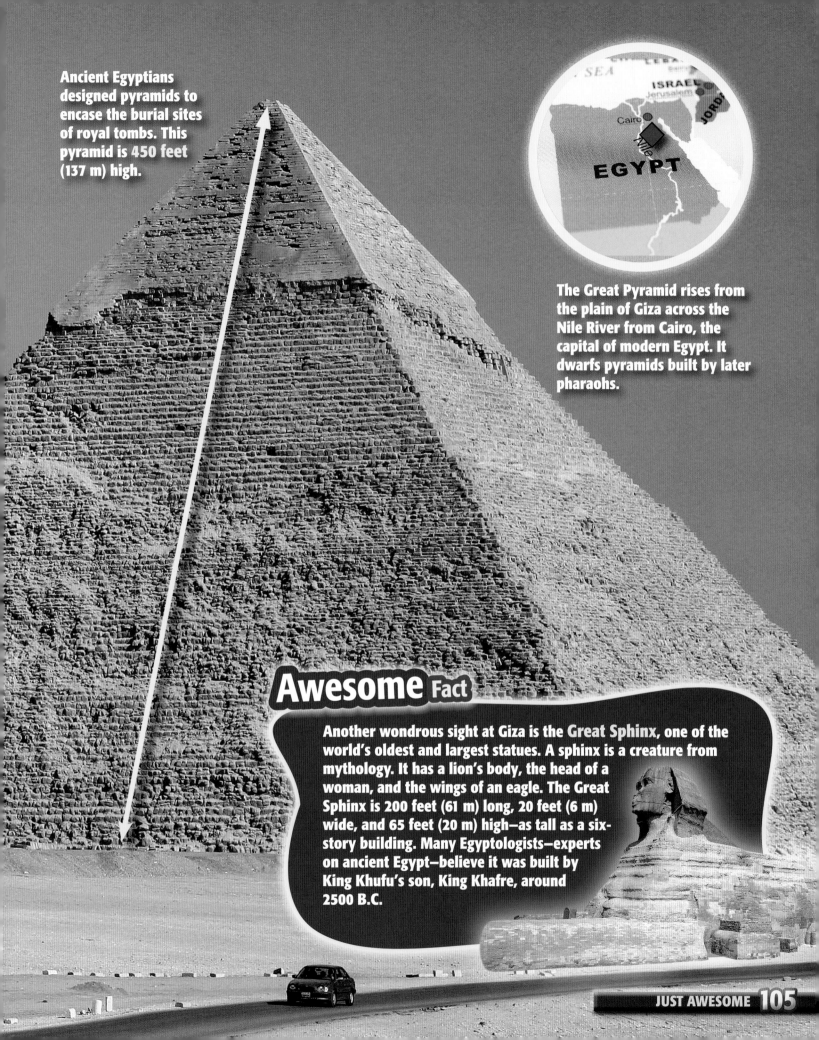

Ancient Egyptians designed pyramids to encase the burial sites of royal tombs. This pyramid is 450 feet (137 m) high.

The Great Pyramid rises from the plain of Giza across the Nile River from Cairo, the capital of modern Egypt. It dwarfs pyramids built by later pharaohs.

Awesome Fact

Another wondrous sight at Giza is the Great Sphinx, one of the world's oldest and largest statues. A sphinx is a creature from mythology. It has a lion's body, the head of a woman, and the wings of an eagle. The Great Sphinx is 200 feet (61 m) long, 20 feet (6 m) wide, and 65 feet (20 m) high—as tall as a six-story building. Many Egyptologists—experts on ancient Egypt—believe it was built by King Khufu's son, King Khafre, around 2500 B.C.

China's Wonderful Wall

Herodotus would probably be thrilled to see the wonders that are the modern world's biggest tourist attractions. **THE GREAT WALL OF CHINA**—the largest man-made structure on Earth—is on the top of everybody's list.

The Great Wall

Construction of the **Great Wall** began 22 centuries ago under the reign of China's first emperor, Shi Huangdi. Most of it was completed between 1368 and 1644, during a period in China's history known as the Ming Dynasty. Today the wall snakes across the land for **1,678 miles** (2,700 km) from east to west. Places where two, three, and even four walls are attached to the central wall push the total length to **6,214 miles** (9,942 km)—1/4th of the Earth's circumference!

Awesome Fact

In China, the Great Wall is called **Wan Li Chang Cheng**. This means "great wall of ten thousand *li*." The li is a measurement of length equal to about 1,640 feet (about half a kilometer).

Prisoners of war and Chinese peasants were forced to build the wall brick by brick. Legend has it that one worker died every time 3 feet (0.9 m) of work was completed.

Watchtowers are built into the wall every 230 feet (70.1 m). Soldiers stationed there were on the lookout for invading armies and workers taking a forbidden break.

The wall is 19 feet (5.8 m) wide at its base and 15 feet (4.6 m) wide at its top. It is nearly 30 feet (9.1 m) high.

Seven
Wonders of the Modern World

STRUCTURE	LOCATION
1. Empire State Building	U.S.
2. The "Chunnel" (Channel Tunnel)	Britain/France
3. Itaipu Dam	Brazil/Paraguay
4. The North Sea Protection Works	The Netherlands
5. Golden Gate Bridge	U.S.
6. CN Tower	Canada
7. Panama Canal	Panama

Spectacular Waterfalls

Hydrologists—scientists who study Earth's water—collect data about cataracts (another name for large, powerful waterfalls). They study the width of the falls, the length of its longest drop (the distance the water has to tumble), and the flow rate (how many cubic feet of water falls every minute).

By most standards, Victoria Falls, on the border of Zimbabwe and Zambia in Africa, is considered to be the largest waterfall in the world—although there are others that are taller or whose water falls at a faster rate.

MALAWI

ZAMBIA

Lusaka ■

Lilongwe ●

■ Harare

ZIMBABWE

Awesome Fact

Victoria Falls is actually made up of five different falls: Rainbow Falls (the highest), Devil's Cataract, Main Falls, Horseshoe Falls, and Eastern Cataract.

Awesome Fact

Mosi-oa-Tunya—"The Mist that Thunders"—is the name of Victoria Falls in the local tribal language. The mist is created by winds that vaporize the water as it swirls down.

In the dry months between September and December, when the river flow is at a low level, fearless tourists can swim right up to the edge of the falls in an area known as the Devil's Pool.

The falls are 5,604 feet (1,708 m) wide—more than a mile across!

The Zambezi River dumps its full volume over a drop of 360 feet (109.8 m) to form the biggest sheet of falling water in the world.

TOP 5
Most Awe-Inspiring Waterfalls

NAME	LOCATION	LONGEST DROP	WIDTH
1. Victoria Falls	Africa	360 feet (110 m)	5,604 feet (1,708 m)
2. Angel Falls	South America	2,647 feet (807 m)	350 feet (107 m)*
3. Iguacu Falls	South America	269 feet (82 m)	8,858 feet (2,700 m)
4. Niagara Falls	North America	167 feet (52 m)	2,600 feet (792 m)
5. Dettifoss	Iceland	144 feet (44 m)	328 feet (100 m)

* Average width   SOURCE: victoriafalls-guide.net

A Watery Life

LAKES are bodies of fresh or salt water surrounded by land. But in some parts of the world, inventive people have figured out how to put land into lakes!

Reedy Residences

Lake Titicaca (tih-tee-*cah*-cah) is home to the Uros tribe, native South American people who used to live in the nearby mountains. More than 500 years ago, the Uros fled to Titicaca to escape the *conquistadors* (con-*key*-sta-doors), Spanish conquerors who were searching for gold and silver. Needing land to build their homes, the Uros learned to make **islands** from the thick totora (toh-*toh*-rah) reeds that grow around the lake. Today, some 2,000 of their descendants live on 42 artificial islands.

A typical home on Inle Lake in Burma

For the Record

Lake Titicaca, 12,500 feet (3,812 m) above sea level on the border between Peru and Bolivia, is the largest freshwater lake in South America.

After harvesting and bundling the totora reeds, the Uros weave them into long rafts that are then attached to living reeds. These rafts are the foundations of small islands that are strong enough to support small buildings. The large reed fish serves a dual purpose—decoration and watchtower.

Villages Afloat

On the other side of the globe is beautiful Inle (*in*-lay) Lake in the Southeast Asian country of Burma (also known as Myanmar). Here, the Inthar people live in more than 17 villages on **artificial islands**, like their ancestors have done for centuries. Using techniques similar to the Uros tribe, the Inthars weave together reeds and water hyacinths, floating plants with thick root systems that help anchor the islands.

Totora reeds are also used for making houses, churches, boats, and watchtowers—even a meal, because you can eat parts of the reed.

Chapter 8
Awesome Space

What do smoke detectors, freeze-dried foods, fogless ski goggles, and flat screen televisions have in common? They are among the many products on Earth that were developed for high-tech missions to **OUTER SPACE**. Space exploration not only inspires useful inventions, it also provides a steady stream of awesome photographs of the galaxy we live in.

In This Chapter

- **Working and Living in Space**
- **The New, Improved Hubble Space Telescope**
- **Amazing Light Shows in the Sky**
- **And Much More...**

For the Record

Clusters of space dust and gases that swirl among constellations of stars are called *nebula*. This composite image of the **CARINA NEBULA**, one of the largest and brightest nebula in the Milky Way, was taken by the Hubble Space Telescope.

Working and Living in Space

When the International Space Station (ISS) is completed in 2011, scientists expect that the research aboard the orbiting laboratory will lead to great discoveries in medicine, technology, and space.

The ISS will be the largest space station ever built. Its construction and upkeep are being supported by the United States and 16 other nations. Astronauts who repair, supply, and improve the ISS mostly travel on the U.S. space shuttle or Russian spacecraft.

ISS travels at 17,210 mph (27,697 kph) as it orbits the Earth 240 miles (386 km) up.

For a very hefty price, Earthlings can join a mission to the space station.

The first part of the station was launched in 1998. Astronauts from many nations have lived and worked on the ISS since November 2, 2000.

Awesome Fact

In 2010, astronauts installed an observation deck on the ISS. The deck has windows all around, giving space station residents awesome views of Earth.

Solar panels harness the sun's energy and power the station.

Earth can be seen below the *Endeavor* which is docked to the ISS.

Floating in space, where everything is weightless, two astronauts can easily move a 1,700-pound (771-kg) tank from the cargo bay of the space shuttle *Endeavor* to the ISS. Although the U.S. will no longer operate space shuttles after 2010, Russian spacecraft will continue to service the station.

ISS023E021088

Zero Gravity, Zero Weight

Whether you weigh 80 pounds or 800 pounds, you'll be light as a feather in space without the Earth's force of gravity to pull you down. Being weightless sounds like fun, but it poses some unusual problems for everyday living that earthbound people never have to think about.

Catch the Hot Sauce

Cosmonaut Yuri I. Malenchenko (left), Expedition 7 Mission Commander, and astronaut Edward T. Lu, NASA ISS science officer and flight engineer, share a meal on board the ISS. Whoever set the table sure left a lot of things up in the air. The hot sauce is hard to catch as it floats by.

Awesome
Dinner Menu

Here's a look at a typical dinner on board the ISS.

Shrimp Cocktail –
Rehydratable
(Water is added)

Beef Steak – Irradiated
(subjected to radiation to kill harmful bacteria)

Rehydratable Fruit Cocktail –
Thermostabilized
(heat processed to kill harmful bacteria)

Strawberry Drink – Beverage

Tea with Lemon – Beverage

Floating Snack

To help keep the ISS crew healthy, fresh fruit is delivered to the station. NASA Science Officer Mike Fincke, of Expedition 9, plans to bite into an apple or two—once he can grab them.

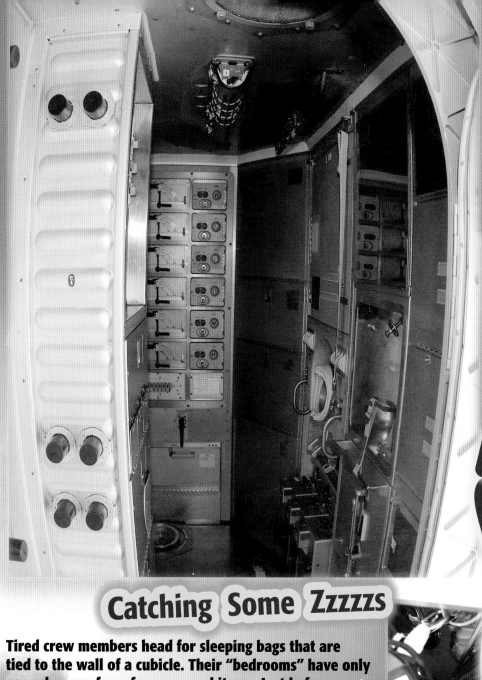

Gotta Go?

When you take your turn in the space toilet, you'll have to strap yourself in. Then you can pee through a special funnel that connects to a tube which flows into a tank. Collected urine is later dispersed into space. Solid waste, which is freeze-dried to kill bacteria, is stored and disposed of after landing.

Awesome Fact

Daily exercise is important on the ISS. It helps the astronauts maintain muscle tone and keeps their bones strong. It also helps them get rid of the "space snuffles," fluid that builds up in their heads. Remember: There's no gravity to pull the mucus downward and make their noses run!

Catching Some Zzzzzs

Tired crew members head for sleeping bags that are tied to the wall of a cubicle. Their "bedrooms" have only enough space for a few personal items. Just before bedtime, astronauts listen to music, watch DVDs, write e-mails home, or transmit their thoughts on ham radios.

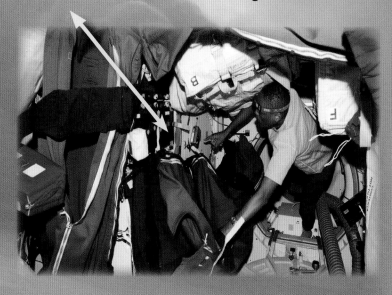

Heavenly Sights

Most nights, if the sky is clear, we can look up and see twinkling stars and the moon. If we're lucky enough to be at the right place at the right time, we get to see a spectacular light show produced by Mother Nature.

Northern Lights

The Cree Nation, one of the largest tribes in Canada, calls them "The Dance of the Spirits." That's a good description. The Northern Lights, also known by the Latin name Aurora Borealis (uh-*roar*-uh bore-ee-*al*-iss), often look like a colorful swirl of movement in the sky.

Alaska Sky-Show

Head north to Alaska where you are likely to see the Northern Lights from December to March when the nights are longest. Sometimes the show lasts all night. But at other times, it's over in a few minutes. Check the Internet for information about where and when to see the Northern Lights this year. Maybe one day you'll be lucky enough to see them in person.

Scientists believe that the Northern Lights are created by weather conditions in space. They may begin with solar activity or space storms that send electrically-charged particles toward Earth. The charged particles crash into gaseous particles in the Earth's magnetic field and are pulled up toward the North Pole. These electromagnetic collisions produce glowing patterns of red and green lights in the sky.

Showers of Light

You don't need a telescope, just watchful eyes and patience, to see meteors streak across the sky. The best viewing place is somewhere far from the glow of city lights.

Once in a while, chunks of asteroids called meteorites land on Earth. The Hoba meteorite, the largest ever found on Earth, weighs about 60 tons. Discovered in 1920 on a farm in the African nation of Namibia, it is believed to be at least 200 million years old.

Awesome Fact

A meteor is the word scientists use to describe the light made by a meteoroid—usually a small piece of an asteroid—as it enters Earth's atmosphere and explodes into a ball of fire. The bright streaks of light made by meteoroids are also known as falling stars.

Fixing It in Space

In 2009, astronauts from the space shuttle completed a $1 billion mission to repair the orbiting Hubble Space Telescope which was launched in 1990. Now the Hubble is better than ever, sending near-perfect photos of space back to Earth. Take a look at some of them.

Hello, Hubble

A Star Is Born

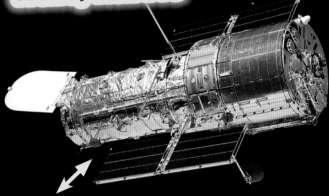

The Hubble Space Telescope gets its power from the sun, using two 25-foot (7.5-m) solar panels. Hubble orbits the Earth every 97 minutes.

Tricky Repairs

This image shows a pillar containing newly forming stars in the Carina Nebula. A nebula is a cloud of gas and dust around stars.

During its repair mission, a shuttle crew carefully installed two new cameras and replaced Hubble's broken parts. New light-sensitive instruments make Hubble's photos clearer than ever.

Crowded Cluster

This shot shows a cluster that has nearly 10 million stars. ←→

From TIME FOR KIDS Magazine

Impact!

A "bruise" on Jupiter—the dark smudge at the bottom right—is the result of a recent collision with a comet or asteroid. →

Galileo built this telescope. He made many discoveries with it.

Galileo's Vision

Four hundred years ago, the great astronomer Galileo Galilei (ga-lih-*lay*-oh ga-lih-*lay*), born in Italy in 1564, became the first person to turn his telescope toward the sky. Although his telescope was small and the view was blurry, his discoveries changed astronomy forever. Galileo built his first telescope in 1609, using two pieces of carved wood held together with copper wire, leather, and paper. Through it he saw detailed views of Earth's moon and the planets, including Mars. He is also credited with discovering four of Jupiter's moons and finding that the Milky Way is a collection of stars.

Butterfly Nebula

One of the first photos taken in 2009 by the new, improved Hubble is this dying star with glowing "wings."

Now There Is One

In 2003, NASA sent Spirit and Opportunity, twin Exploration Rovers, to Mars. Since then, the two robots have been sending back amazing photographs of the Red Planet and collecting valuable information about its climate and geology. In 2009, Spirit got stuck on the planet's sandy surface and stopped moving around.

A special camera on top of each Rover takes 360-degree photographs.

Capture-Filter Magnets collect magnetic dust for scientists to analyze.

The High Gain Antenna beams information back to Earth.

Like mechanical geologists, the Rovers use special science instruments, among other tools, to study rocks and soil on the planet's surface.

The mobility system keeps the Rover balanced as it moves over rough terrain.

Look carefully at this panoramic photograph of the Martian landscape taken by Spirit's camera. You can see the robot's tracks leading to the place where it sunk into sandy ground.

Awesome Fact

The goals of the Rover mission are to help scientists:
- Determine whether there were ever tiny life forms, such as microbes, on Mars
- Learn about the climate of Mars
- Learn about the geology of Mars
- See if Mars could be used as a base to explore other areas of space

Source: NASA

Through the work of the Rovers, scientists have found widespread deposits of salts and minerals on Mars. What's exciting about this discovery is that the salts and minerals needed water to form! At one time, scientists conclude, there must have been enough water on the Red Planet to sustain life.

It may be grounded forever, but Spirit still sends photographs and data back to Earth. Scientists hope to devise new tasks for the robot that can be done from its fixed position.

New Stars of the Milky Way

This beautiful image was taken by an infrared space camera–the **SPITZER SPACE TELESCOPE**. It shows a new population of huge stars forming inside the **MILKY WAY GALAXY**.

Scientists believe that in the center of the Milky Way is a humongous black hole that will swallow anything that comes its way. They think of a black hole as a kind of bottomless pit. Black holes are thought to be so deep that no light can escape from them.

The Milky Way is Earth's home galaxy–a group of more than 100 billion stars held together by gravity and other forces and surrounded by mysterious dark matter.

A star is a dense ball of hot, glowing gas that sends out waves of energy, mostly in the form of light. Scientists are still trying to figure out what goes on deep inside of stars.

The distance it takes for the light of a star to travel to Earth is measured in light years.

By the time we can see a new star, it has already been in space for millions, if not billions, of Earth years. That's because it takes so long for the distant star's light to reach our planet. So the "new" stars in this image are really very old.

Awesome Fact

Astronomers are now in the process of remapping the Milky Way using a radio telescope called VLBA. Through its 10 radio-telescope antennas that stretch from Hawaii to New England and the Caribbean, VLBA can take images of space that are hundreds of times sharper than those taken by the Hubble Space Telescope!

Light travels at 186,000 miles (300,000 km) per second. To figure out how far light can travel in a year, do the math (hint: it's in the trillions of miles): 186,000 miles/second x 60 seconds (1 minute) x 60 minutes (1 hour) x 24 hours (1 day) x 365 days (1 year) = 5,865,696,000,000 miles/year (9,460,800,000,000 km)

When a star begins to die, it first grows to an enormous size. Then it collapses into a dense ball called a white dwarf. It may take billions of years for the white dwarf to cool down and disappear.

Chapter 9

AweSome

Weather

& Other Forces of Nature

Earthquakes, volcanoes, avalanches, and other physical events are Earth's means of building mountains, carving out lakes, and making new landscapes. To most humans, though, these acts of nature are forces that destroy lives and cause enormous damage. Our challenge is to learn how to protect ourselves from these unavoidable events.

In This Chapter

- Erupting Volcanoes
- Melting Glaciers
- Trembling Earthquakes
- And Much More...

Awesome Fact

By 2100, polar bears in the Arctic could die out, and the region's icebergs and GLACIERS may disappear.

Awesome Fact

Residents of Haiti, in the Caribbean, and Chile, in South America, are rebuilding their countries after powerful **EARTHQUAKES** struck their homelands in early 2010.

Awesome Fact

There are more than 1,500 active **VOLCANOES** on the surface of the Earth.

Winterlands

People who live in snowy climates know that the fluffy white stuff is beautiful but can also be dangerous.

TOP 5
Snowiest Places in the U.S.

CITY	STATE	AVERAGE SNOWFALL PER YEAR
1. Paradise	Washington	676 inches (1,717 cm)
2. Mount Baker	Washington	647 inches (1,643 cm)
3. Valdez	Alaska	326 inches (828 cm)
4. Mount Washington	New Hampshire	261 inches (663 cm)
5. Blue Canyon	California	240 inches (610 cm)

The snowiest place in the U.S—Paradise, Washington—is located in Mount Rainier National Park, 5,400 feet (1,646 m) up the southern slope of the mountain.

Deadly Snow

An **avalanche** is a skier's greatest enemy. Under the right conditions, a giant wall of snow tumbles at high speed down steep slopes, burying everything in its path. There are many reasons for avalanches, including: heavy snowstorms, earthquakes, thunder or other loud noises, temperature changes, falling rocks or ice, even snowmobilers or skiers whose sounds or movements loosen large sections of snow.

For the Record

Huascarán (wah-scah-*rahn*), the tallest peak in Peru, is the site of the one of the largest avalanches in recent history. In 1962, an earthquake caused a giant wall of ice, snow, and rocks to roar 13,900 feet (4,237 m) down the mountainside. The avalanche traveled nine miles (14 km), destroying trees, livestock, and villages, and killing thousands of people in its deadly path.

Awesome Facts

● There are three stages to an avalanche. First, loose snow starts to slide down the slope, usually with a "whumping" sound. Second, the snow gathers speed as it follows a path called the "avalanche track." Third, the snow comes to a halt in what's known as the "runout zone."

● Ski resorts often set off controlled explosive charges to trigger small avalanches and prevent larger ones from taking place and endangering skiers.

Earth-shaking News

Several million times a year, slabs of soil and rock below the Earth's surface come apart or crash into each other and produce an earthquake—a sudden release of energy that causes the Earth's crust to tremble and shake. Most of these quakes are harmless, but sometimes, if the shaking is powerful enough, an earthquake can destroy whole cities.

Bone-chilling Quake

One of the biggest earthquakes ever recorded rattled the South American country of Chile on February 27, 2010. The epicenter of the quake was just offshore in the Pacific Ocean. Hundreds of Chileans were killed by the quake and by the huge waves that followed it.

Over half a million homes were damaged by the 2010 earthquake in Chile. On this street in Concepcion City, few buildings remained standing.

On January 12, 2010, a powerful quake practically destroyed Port-au-Prince, the capital of Haiti, a country in the Caribbean Sea. Officials estimated that 200,000 Haitians died and 250,000 others were injured. More than 1.5 million people were left without homes and basic necessities.

What Happens During an Earthquake

The Earth's crust is not solid. It is made up of pieces that slowly shift. A fault line is a place below the surface where two pieces meet. An earthquake is the sudden release of energy along the fault line as rocks break in response to stress. There are different types of quakes, depending on the kind of movement along the fault. Haiti was rocked by a strike-slip earthquake, in which one side of the fault slides horizontally past the other.

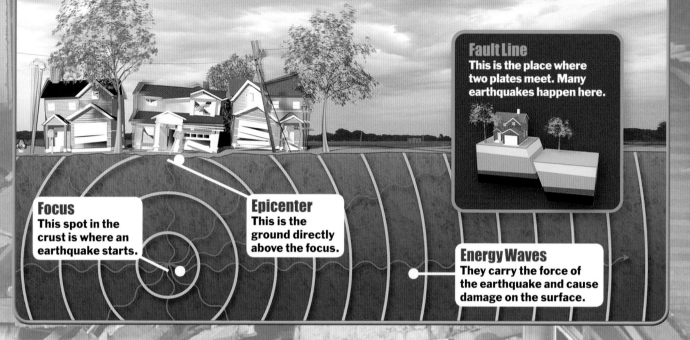

Fault Line
This is the place where two plates meet. Many earthquakes happen here.

Focus
This spot in the crust is where an earthquake starts.

Epicenter
This is the ground directly above the focus.

Energy Waves
They carry the force of the earthquake and cause damage on the surface.

Awesome Fact

There are several ways to measure the magnitude, or force, of an earthquake. One of them, the "Richter Scale," is based on formulas developed by an American mathematician, Charles Richter, in 1935. Richter used an instrument to measure the size of ground waves created by an earthquake and then calculated a number to represent the earthquake's power. Earthquakes that register below 4.0 on the Richter Scale are usually mild. Quakes above 5.0 can cause terrible damage.

TOP 5 Earthquakes

The earthquake that hit Chile on February 27 was one of the most powerful ever recorded. It had a magnitude of 8.8. This list shows the largest earthquakes since 1900.

② **Prince William Sound, Alaska**
9.2 magnitude, 1964

④ **Kamchatka Peninsula, Russia**
9.0 magnitude, 1952

⑤ **Off the coast of Ecuador**
8.8 magnitude, 1906

③ **Off the coast of northern Sumatra**
9.1 magnitude, 2004

① **Chile** 9.5 magnitude, 1960
⑤ **Off the coast of Chile**
8.8 magnitude, 2010

Twister Alert!

In *The Wizard of Oz*, a tornado, or twister, carries a young girl and her dog to a magical place. In real life tornadoes rip up the ground, killing people and flattening buildings.

Heads Up!

If you see a dark or greenish sky, a wall-like cloud, and large hail, and if you hear a loud roar coming from the sky—a tornado may be heading your way! You should quickly find shelter in a basement or lowest floor of a building and stay clear of corners, windows, and doors.

Storming the Earth

Tornadoes are twisting columns of wind that can reach speeds of 318 mph (512 kmph). At that velocity, or speed, they can lift cars into the air, rip whole houses from their foundations, and damage steel-and-concrete buildings.

TOP 5 Tornado States

About 800 tornadoes are reported in the U.S. each year, mostly east of the Rocky Mountains during spring and summer. Many of these twisters strike a group of states in an area called **Tornado Alley**, which extends north from Texas to South Dakota. The numbers on the map show, on average, how many tornadoes strike each state every year.

3 Kansas 55
4 Nebraska 45
5 Iowa 37
2 Oklahoma 57
1 Texas 139
3 Florida 55

KEY
☐ Area most hit by tornadoes
☐ Top states for tornadoes

Tornadoes in Space

Astronomers are watching the skies for tornadoes—the skies of deep space, that is! Space tornadoes are funnel-shaped, like those on Earth, but they travel much faster, at a speed of one million miles per hour (1.6 million kmph). Scientists suspect that these windstorms are connected to the formation of new stars. They also think that space tornadoes are the electromagnetic forces that cause the Northern and Southern Lights—where the night skies turn shades of green and red.

Awesome Fact

Every three hours a tornado forms in space. It only takes one minute for the tornado to reach Earth's ionosphere— the area that lies between 62 and 250 miles (100 and 402 km) above the ground. There, tornadoes release their energy and make space dust glow. It's the glow that gives us the Northern or Southern lights. Space tornadoes are not dangerous to humans, but like any storm, they can damage electrical equipment.

What's the Climate?

Cold, hot, wet, dry, temperate: Earth has many different climates, each supporting different kinds of plant and animal life. The ocean covers a little over two-thirds of our planet. That doesn't leave much land for humans, but what's left has many record-setting environments.

On July 10, 1914, **DEATH VALLEY** had the highest temperature ever recorded in the United States: 134°F (57°C). During summer, temperatures can easily hit a toasty 120°F (49°C).

MOUNT WAI'ALE'ALE, KAUAI, HAWAII

Rain falls on this 5,148-foot-high (1,569 m) mountain between 335 and 360 days a year, for a total of 460-512 inches (1,168-1,300 cm).

Less than one inch of rain falls on the rocks and dunes of the **ATACAMA DESERT,** a 600 mile (960 km) strip of land in northern Chile and southern Peru. In some parts of the desert, nothing can grow—not even bacteria.

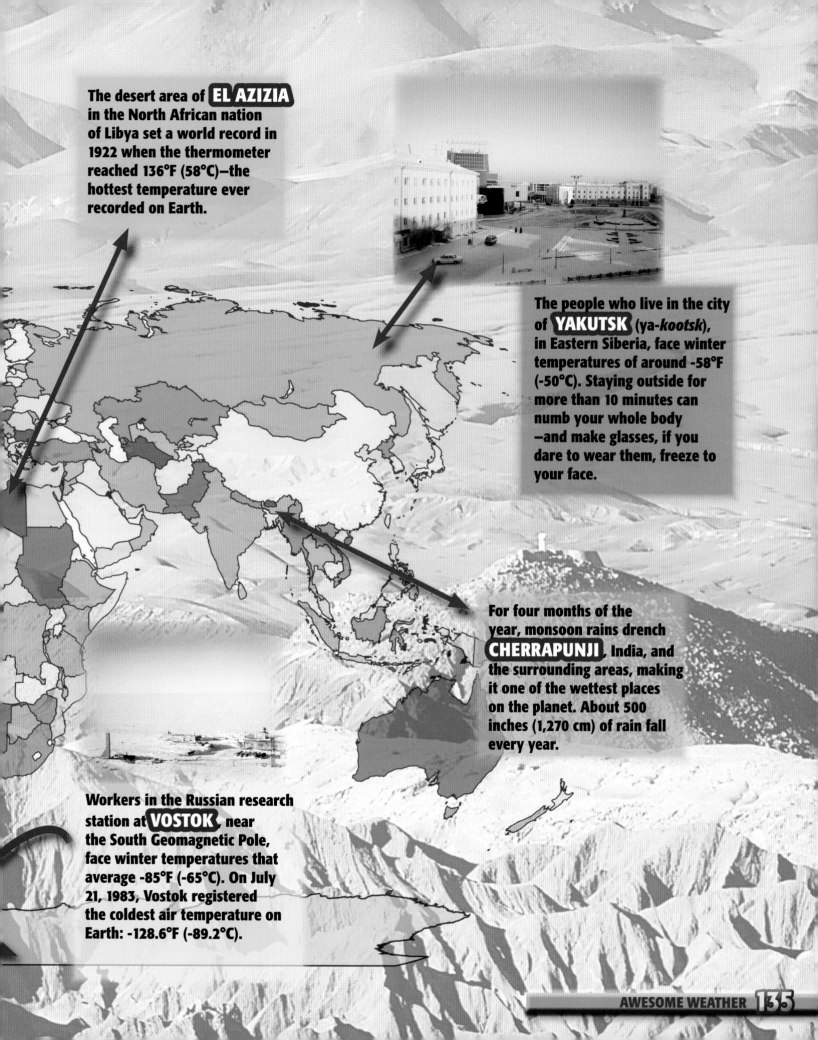

The desert area of **EL AZIZIA** in the North African nation of Libya set a world record in 1922 when the thermometer reached 136°F (58°C)—the hottest temperature ever recorded on Earth.

The people who live in the city of **YAKUTSK** (ya-*kootsk*), in Eastern Siberia, face winter temperatures of around -58°F (-50°C). Staying outside for more than 10 minutes can numb your whole body —and make glasses, if you dare to wear them, freeze to your face.

For four months of the year, monsoon rains drench **CHERRAPUNJI**, India, and the surrounding areas, making it one of the wettest places on the planet. About 500 inches (1,270 cm) of rain fall every year.

Workers in the Russian research station at **VOSTOK**, near the South Geomagnetic Pole, face winter temperatures that average -85°F (-65°C). On July 21, 1983, Vostok registered the coldest air temperature on Earth: -128.6°F (-89.2°C).

Volcano Power

Hawaiians joke that their famous volcano, Kilauea (kill-uh-*way*-ah), adds more real estate, or sellable land, to their island every year. That's no jest: Hot lava flowing from any erupting volcano eventually cools and forms new cliffs, plains, and mountains. The activity of volcanoes shows us one of the ways the Earth's crust has been shaped for billions of years.

Blowing Its Top

A volcano erupts when magma—hot liquid rock bottled up deep inside the Earth—reaches a bursting point and explodes into the air, turning into fiery lava and tephra (*teff*-ra)—a cloud of ash, cinders, and rock.

TOP 5
World's Tallest Volcanoes

NAME	LOCATION	HEIGHT
1. Ojos del Salado	Argentina/Chile	22,595 ft (6,887 m)
2. Llullaillaco	Argentina/Chile	22,057 ft (6,723 m)
3. Tipas	Argentina	21,850 ft (6,660 m)
4. Cerro El Condor	Argentina	21,430 ft (6,532 m)
5. Coropuma	Peru	20,922 ft (6,377 m)

Source: http://www.1iverating.com/top/1021/

For the Record

There are more than 1,500 active volcanoes on the surface of the Earth.

For the Record

In 2010, a volcano in Iceland erupted, spewing thick ash into the air. As a result, planes to and from nearby Europe had to be grounded. Millions of travelers were stranded for more than a week as the airlines waited for the ash to clear.

Awesome Facts

- The most common type of volcanic activity on our planet happens underneath the ocean. At least three-quarters of the lava erupted on Earth each year comes from volcanoes on the deep sea floor.

- Molten lava reaches temperatures of 1,300-2,000°F (704-1,093°C).

No Chance of Rain

Unlike sudden earthquakes or floods, **DROUGHTS** develop slowly. Long periods without rain dry up water supplies, turn dirt to dust, and can destroy civilizations. Scientists believe that the Mayas of Central America and the Anasazi Indian tribes of the U.S. southwest were the victims of terrible droughts.

In 1935, during one of the worst droughts in American history, an enormous cloud of dust swoops across the Plains.

America's Dust Bowl

One of the worst droughts in U.S. history took place between 1930 and 1940 in the states of Texas, Oklahoma, and other parts of the Great Plains. Years of poor farming practices in the region had left the soil unprotected from heat, wind, and erosion. The drought made everything worse. Without rain, the topsoil turned to dust that blew across the land in huge clouds, burying homes, roads, and fields. As a result, millions of people from the "Dust Bowl" had to leave their farms and look for work in other parts of the country.

Blast from the Past

EYEWITNESS TO THE DUST BOWL

On July 10, 1933, a TIME magazine reporter traveling through the Dust Bowl described a wasteland invaded by starving insects.

Date: July 10, 1933

...(I)n Indiana there were cracks in the earth an inch wide. Motorists in Grundy County, Illinois, saw chinch bugs in ribbons 100 ft. wide in the roads. The bugs were eating their way from field to field. North Dakota's drought brought out a destructive swarm of grasshoppers. In Southwest Kansas fiery winds blew so much shifting topsoil from the fields that snow-plows had to be used to clear the highways.

April 1936, brings no spring rains to Texas—rather, a huge dust storm that buries everything in its path.

A Family Story

An American writer, John Steinbeck, turned his impressions of the Dust Bowl into a great novel, *The Grapes of Wrath*, published in 1939. The book tells the story of the Joads, a family from Oklahoma who are driven from their farm by the drought and endure many hardships on their way to California to find work.

The Big Meltdown

Today, nearly all scientists believe the temperature of Earth is heating up, and life on the planet as we know it may be at risk. Why do experts conclude this is happening? For one thing, they are seeing huge glaciers and icebergs around the world starting to melt away.

Compare the Shepherd Glacier in Montana as it was in 1913 (top photo) with how it looked in 2005. As glaciers shrink, so does our water supply. That affects all forms of life on our planet.

1913

2005

Awesome Facts

● Glaciers are frozen rivers of ice that store about 75% of the world's supply of fresh water.

● If all the land glaciers in the world were to melt, the water they release could raise ocean levels by more than 230 feet (70 m). Rising sea levels, in turn, might mean that some coastlines and other low-lying places on Earth would end up underwater.

Awesome Fact

Most scientists agree that one of the main causes of global warming is the rapid increase in levels of carbon dioxide (CO_2), a heat-trapping gas in the Earth's atmosphere. This increase is almost entirely due to human activities, such as:

● Burning coal and other fossil fuels in power plants and factories that pollute the atmosphere with carbon dioxide

● Using cars, trucks, and other vehicles that burn gasoline and release carbon dioxide

● Cutting down forests that, if left standing, would help remove carbon dioxide from the atmosphere.

As glaciers and icebergs melt, penguins, polar bears, and other animals that live in ice- and snow-covered regions are seeing their habitats disappear.

Five
Things You Can Do to Reduce Carbon Dioxide

1. Plant a Tree ⟶ More trees help the Earth!

2. Take Shorter Showers ⟶ Two thirds of all heating costs are due to showers. Heat produced by fossil fuels adds CO_2 to the air.

3. Buy Local Products ⟶ Delivery trucks that drive shorter distances pollute less!

4. Use a Reusable Bottle for Water, Juice, or Other Drinks You Carry ⟶ It takes energy to make the plastic in throwaway bottles. And it takes even more energy to get rid of the 2.5 million bottles that are tossed away every hour in the U.S.

5. Fill the Dishwasher ⟶ Running the dishwasher only when it's full reduces use of electricity and water.

Chapter 10

Awesome Collections

Almost everybody collects something. Some people collect valuable objects, like paintings or antique cars. Others collect everyday items, from books to baseball caps. Still others collect more unusual things, like hair from celebrities. But whether the items in it are common or a little kooky, collections are cool.

In This Chapter

- Loads of Lint
- Icy Marvels
- A Spy Museum
- And Much More…

Awesome Fact

Some collectors buy bananas for what's on the peel, not what's inside!

For the Record

A museum in Burlingame, California, has the world's biggest PEZ™ dispenser! This dispenser is 7 feet, 10 inches tall.

Awesome Fact

There's a word for a person who collects sugar packets—sucrologist!

Kooky Collections

Most collectors spend a lot of time hunting for their favorite items—in ads, in flea markets, on the Internet, or in junk stores. Others prefer to collect stuff that is much closer to home!

Pounds of Postage

Visitors to Boys Town, Nebraska, don't want to miss the 600-pound (273 kg) ball of 4,655,000 postage stamps put together by the local stamp collecting club in the 1950s. The young club members spent six months sticking together canceled stamps around a golf-ball core. A lot of kids have stamp collections, but they can't lick this one!

Awesome Fact

A philatelist is a person who collects stamps. The "phila" part of the word comes from the Greek word *philos*, which means loving. Bibliophiles love books. Cinephiles love movies. And arctophiles love to collect teddy bears!

Loads of Lint

No one has more belly button lint than Graham Barker. Since 1984, he has probably collected more navel lint, or fluff, than anyone in the world. Barker says his collection is special because a) probably no one else even has a lint collection, b) definitely no one has a collection of Barker's lint, and c) Barker has collected lint from his navel every day, so his collection is complete. The entire collection sits in three glass jars. That's not a lot, but, after all, a belly button doesn't really hold that much fuzz.

Top Bananas

People don't give much thought to tossing banana peels in the trash—unless they're Banana Peel Label collectors. Their passion is to save thousands of those colorful little stickies on the peels, each with a different design. And while the collectors are at it, they can learn a bit about geography. Did you know that Ecuador, in South America, is the world's biggest exporter of bananas—with 600 different labels to prove it?

Sweet Thoughts

The first thing some collectors do when they go out to eat is examine the sugar packets on the table. One man in England has gathered more than 8,000 packets since he started collecting in 1978! He has also organized them into different categories, depending on the packet design: Airlines, Hotels, Burger Places, U.S. Presidents, and so on. And he's not alone: There is a whole network of sucrologists—people who collect sucrose, or sugar, and trade packets with each other.

Collections Central

Some collections are so big or so amazing, there's no way to enjoy them unless they're on public display in a museum.

Spy vs. Spy

What's it like to be a spy? You'll learn the sneaky tricks of the trade at the **International Spy Museum** in Washington, D.C. Visitors are given a fake identity and a mission to accomplish as they survey more than 600 exhibits about disguises, secret weapons, and hair-raising stories of espionage.

CONFIDENTIAL

Frozen Display

Where else but in America's coldest state would there be a museum that's all about ice—The Fairbanks Ice Museum in Fairbanks, Alaska. Inside a special refrigerated area are sculptures carved from huge blocks of clear-as-crystal Fairbanks ice, weighing over five tons each. Many of the sculptures are created during the World Ice Art Championships, held in Fairbanks every March.

Pez Aplenty

PEZ™ candies are tasty, for sure. But the real reason many people buy them is because they come in those nifty little dispensers topped with the head of a famous movie or cartoon character. At the Burlingame Museum of Pez Memorabilia in Burlingame, California, visitors can see hundreds of amazing dispensers, old and new. The star attraction is the Mickey Mouse Pez, made in 1952. Other popular Pezzes include: Mary Poppins, E.T., Batman, Wonder Woman, and a set of Pirates of the Caribbean!

TOP 5
Favorite U.S. Museums for Kids and Families

MUSEUM	LOCATION	WHAT TO SEE
1. American Museum of Natural History:	NYC, NY	Hayden Planetarium
2. Art Institute of Chicago:	Chicago, IL	Great art from past to present
3. Charles M. Schulz Museum:	Santa Rosa, CA	All about Peanuts cartoons and their creator
4. Experience Music Project:	Seattle, WA	Cool interactive exhibits about pop stars and science fiction writers
5. Exploratorium:	San Francisco, CA	Hands-on exhibits about science from A to Z

Source: http://www.museumstuff.com

Chapter 11
Awesome Jobs

"What do you want to be when you grow up?" is a common question kids are asked. Of course, the answer is up to you. So keep in mind that there are hundreds of jobs in the world of work that might be worth mentioning next time somebody asks you. To get you going, here are some really unusual jobs to think about!

In This Chapter

- Elephant Toenail Clipper
- Movie Sound Effects Artist
- Bird Migration Helper
- And Much More...

Awesome Fact

A pet-food taster in England says his favorite dish is an organic chicken and vegetable dinner for cats!

For the Record

In September 2009, a college graduate from California set out to hold down 50 one-week jobs in one year. He would work at one job in each state and each job would be in an industry the state was known for. In Wisconsin, known for its fine cheese, he worked as a cheese maker. In Utah, known for its beautiful national parks, he worked as a park ranger.

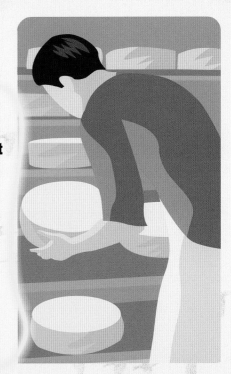

Awesome Fact

According to a U.S. survey, the top five occupations that make workers happiest are:

TOP 5 Occupations

1. Clergy (religious leaders)
2. Firefighter
3. Physical Therapist
4. Author
5. Teacher

Source: http://www.msnbc.msn.com/id/29391533

From TIME FOR KIDS Magazine

Doctor, Lawyer, Merchant, Chief? No Thanks!

If the usual careers don't appeal to you, there are plenty of others that are highly unusual—and unusually cool!

The Sweetest Job of All

Does your sweet tooth rule your life? Think about being a professional chocolate taster, like Rose Potts who works for a chocolate maker in Pennsylvania. Each morning Potts prepares product samples to taste with a group of co-workers. They look at the color of the chocolate, smell it, and feel how it melts in the mouth. They listen to the sound it makes and decide if it's fruity or nutty or spicy. When they're done, they decide if each piece of chocolate tastes right—or if it has to be changed to make it taste better.

How did Potts get started in her job? "I have always liked experimenting with food and I have always liked science. That's how I started on my path as a chocolate taster," says Potts.

Awesome Fact

Chocolate comes from the cocoa bean and most of the world's cocoa bean crops come from West Africa. Cocoa is also grown in South America, Indonesia, and other warm places. Cocoa beans from different regions have different flavors. The beans are made into products like liquid chocolate, chocolate bars, and cocoa powder.

Leader of the flock: A plane guides endangered cranes to their winter home.

Flight School

If you dream of flying like a bird, train to be a pilot for Operation Migration. Since 2001, the group has been rescuing whooping cranes. The cranes are the tallest birds in North America. They are also a species on the edge of dying out.

Operation Migration has several ways to help the cranes. First, they hire trainers to raise chicks. The trainers wear crane costumes so the chicks will not get used to humans. Then they teach cranes to follow an ultra-light plane on a migration route from a bird refuge in Wisconsin to their winter home in Florida. "Birds taught us the art of flying," Operation Migration pilot Joe Duff told TFK. "Now they need our help."

In 1940, only 15 whooping cranes remained in the world. Today, there are about 350 of these magnificent birds. Thanks to groups like Operation Migration, the cranes are making a comeback!

Not Your Usual Job

Some people might say that a few jobs from long ago are pretty weird. Oracles, or fortune tellers, in ancient Greece "read" animal intestines to predict the future. Palace food tasters in the Middle Ages made sure there was no poison in the royal dinner. But even today, if you dare to do something truly different, you can still find work that will make people say "You do what???"

Elephant Pedicurist

Occasionally, elephants in zoos need their nails trimmed, and somebody's got to do it. So how do you give a six-ton elephant a pedicure? First you sedate him—that is, give him a drug that makes him sleep until the job is done. Then using a saw and power grinder, cut, trim, and clip away. But no nail polish, please.

Awesome Facts

● African elephants usually have four toenails on the front feet and three on the back. Asian elephants have five toenails on the front and four on the back.

● An African elephant, the largest living land animal, puts a heavy load on those feet. An adult male can weigh up to 16,500 pounds (7,425 kg). No wonder he's so big: He can eat up to 300 pounds (136 kg) of food in one day!

How do companies that make mouthwash or breath mints know if their product is working? They hire people with sensitive noses who rate other people's stinky breath before—and after—they've used the product.

Gumming Up the Works

Stepping on cast-off chewing gum is really annoying. Luckily, in some cities there are squads of workers who, armed with machines called GumBusters, go forth to remove the sticky wads. With the GumBuster, it takes about five seconds to unstick a piece of gum from the sidewalk.

Such a Nuisance!

In parts of the American South, alligators often squeeze underneath houses or set their sights on eating somebody's dog. Who does the frantic homeowner call? A licensed "nuisance alligator agent" whose job is to catch the reptile with as little fuss as possible. In most states, these agents are the only trappers who have permission to kill the alligators and take their hides and their meat.

Chapter 12
AWESOME
Technology

Without **SCIENCE** and **TECHNOLOGY**, we would be missing so much—from medicines that fight disease to hard-working robots in space. New experiments, inventions, and energy-saving devices that scientists work on today will change the way we live, work, and communicate tomorrow.

For the **Record**

The United States produces enough **HYDROGEN** every year to power as many as 30 million cars equipped with hydrogen fuel cells.

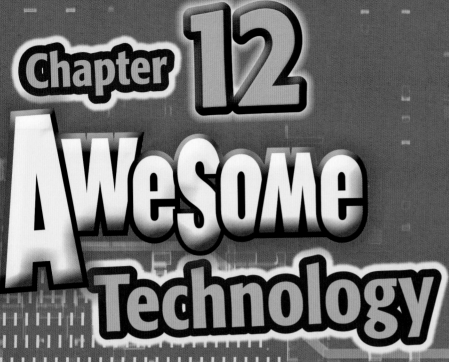

Awesome Fact

A microchip in this **HIGH-TECH EYE** sends images to a blind person's brain.

Awesome Fact

ASIMO, the globe-trotting robot, has conducted a symphony in the U.S., toured England's Windsor Castle, and attended a science fair in Italy.

Awesome Fact

The first **MICROCHIP** was co-invented by two American engineers, Jack Kilby and Robert Noyce, in 1958. Without microchips, almost every electronic device around today, from personal computers to cell phones, wouldn't exist!

Cool Inventions

From TIME FOR KIDS Magazine

Whoever made the first wheel, sometime around 8000 B.C., was one brilliant inventor. What will be the next world-changing invention? Today, with a little help from technology, creative people are designing **INNOVATIVE PRODUCTS** that help solve problems, big and small, and make life a little easier for everybody.

BRIGHT EYES

Scientists at MIT are developing an electric eye that could help the blind to see. A microchip is placed onto the eyeball. Eyeglasses equipped with a camera send images to the chip and then to the brain. Vision won't be perfect, but a person will be able to make out faces and shapes in a room.

A POWERFUL TELESCOPE

The **Herschel Space Observatory** allows scientists to peer deeper into space than ever before. The high-powered telescope sends back images of places in space that have been invisible. For the next three years, Herschel will watch stars and planets being born. And we'll learn more about how the universe came to be.

BEETLE CONTROL

Researchers have created a way to control the flight of beetles by remote control. Cyborg beetles are live bugs that have been implanted with tiny radio antennas and electrical wires. Scientists deliver jolts to the devices, allowing them to pilot the little bugs in different directions.

NEW WAYS TO RIDE

You'll never have to pedal again, thanks to this electronic ride. Honda's U3-X personal mobility device is powered by a rechargeable battery. To steer, simply lean left or right. The U3-X hits a top speed of 3.7 miles per hour (5.9 kmph).

BLAST OFF!

NASA is retiring its current space shuttle fleet in 2010. And the agency is already testing its next line of rockets, including the 327-foot (98-m) **Ares 1 rocket.** It is equipped with improved computers and better engines, giving it more reliability and power. Ares 1 could be taking astronauts out of Earth's orbit by 2015.

STEAM-POWERED CAR

In 2009, Charles Burnett III broke a century-old record: the fastest land speed for a steam-powered car. Burnett was clocked at 151 miles per hour (243 kmph) on a track in California. The 25-foot-long (7.5-meter-long) British steam car has 12 boilers. Its nickname is "the fastest kettle in the world."

Fast Operators

SUPERCOMPUTERS are the world's most powerful computers, capable of processing huge amounts of information at the same time and at lightning speed. If you're hoping for your own supercomputer, you may have to wait a while. Every year, new models of home computers pick up speed and memory power—but for now, they still can't keep up with the superstars.

Jaguar Power

The **Cray XT5 Jaguar** is one of the fastest supercomputers in the world. It can perform over two thousand trillion (2,000,000,000,000,000,000,000) calculations per second! The whole Cray Jaguar system is slightly larger than an NBA basketball court. It takes 6,000 miles (9,656 km) of cables to connect its processors.

Awesome Fact

An average desktop computer can perform about 100 million instructions per second.

Scientists use **supercomputers** like the Cray or the Kraken to perform complicated math problems involving enormous amounts of data. Solving some of these problems helps them understand climate change, nuclear energy, and other important areas of science. By using supercomputers, for example, specialists can develop a forecast of weather patterns for the next 100 years!

Computer Brain

Without the **microprocessor**, a computer simply can't compute. These tiny chips contain all the "brains" the computer needs to process millions of pieces of information every second.

Actual Size

INCHES 1

The Jaguar uses 45,376 microprocessors working together on a single problem. Most home computers have one microprocessor.

Awesome Facts

● Just as the speed of a car is measured in miles per hour (mph), the speed of a supercomputer's response to a command is measured in FLOPS—**F**loating **P**oint **O**perations **P**er **S**econd. The number of FLOPS tells how fast the computer can obey instructions from the user.

● A basic calculator performs at only 10 FLOPS.

● The fastest supercomputers today can perform at a rate of several PFLOPS (P is for Peta). One PETAFLOP equals one quadrillion (or 1,000 trillion) FLOPS.

Blast from the Past

Deep Blue, a special-purpose supercomputer, was developed by IBM specifically to play chess. In 1996, Deep Blue challenged the world chess champion, Gary Kasparov, to a six-game match. Deep Blue won the first game, but Kasparov won the match, 4-2. A year later, after being reprogrammed, Deep Blue won a rematch with Kasparov by one game—and then Deep Blue retired.

TOP 5 Supercomputers

COMPUTER	SPEED (MEASURED IN FLOPS)	LOCATION
1. Cray XT5 Jaguar	1.75 PFLOPS*	U.S.
2. IBM Roadrunner	1.05 PFLOPS	U.S.
3. Kraken	832 TFLOPS**	U.S.
4. Jugene	825.5 TFLOPS	Germany
5. Tianhe-1	563.1 TFLOPS	China

* P is for Peta = one quadrillion, or 1,000 trillion   ** T is for Tera = one trillion

Source: http://www.top500.org/lists/2009/11

Computer Pests

Like a **WORM** in an apple, a nasty computer program can burrow into a PC and eat through its files, doing lots of damage along the way. Many invading programs, called malware, are invented by malicious, or mean-spirited, computer hackers. Luckily, there are lots of ways to fight the invaders, but you should always be on the alert!

Wicked Worms

In schools and offices, many computers are connected to each other. Computer programs called **"worms"** can sneak into these computer networks, automatically infecting the whole system before anyone is aware. One of the nastiest things a worm does is find e-mail addresses and send copies of itself to all of the people on the list!

Awesome Fact

Unlike worms, computer viruses can't infect a computer network on their own but are usually passed on through e-mail or through a website. Once a virus takes hold, it turns computer files into "zombies" by changing their instructional code and directing them to do hateful things—like making it impossible to shut down the computer without pulling the plug.

Most Visited ▾   Getting Started   Latest Headlines

 facebook

Does the word "koobface" remind you of something? If you guessed that it's a scrambled version of Facebook, you're right. It's also the name of a worm that, since 2008, has spread through Facebook, My Space, and other social networking sites. Because of the way it is programmed, the worm only attacks computers with Windows operating systems.

Consumer Reports, a magazine that writes about all kinds of products, calculated that the damage done by computer viruses in 2008 cost consumers 8.5 billion dollars.

Sneaky Spies

Is your computer spying on you? It probably is—and so far, that's not against the law. **Spyware** programs secretly install themselves on your computer, collect information, and send it over the Internet to someone else. Usually what the "spies" want to know is what sites you often visit and what kinds of things you like so they can send you advertisements about stuff that you'd be tempted to buy.

TOP 5
Ways to Spot Spyware

1. The computer works very slowly because spyware programs are using up memory
2. Bookmarks change mysteriously
3. Ads pop up from unknown sites that know your name
4. Ads pop up even when you're offline
5. Your Home Page setting is replaced by another site

Hackers, the people who break into computer systems and spread viruses and worms, aren't just nasty—they're criminals. In 1999, one of the earliest hackers sent a virus called Melissa over the Internet to more than one million e-mail addresses. The hacker was sentenced to 20 months in jail and fined $5,000.

TOP 5
Ways to Protect Your Computer

1. Install anti-virus and spyware removal programs on your computer
2. Update these programs regularly to protect against new infections
3. Scan your computer regularly and delete infected files
4. Don't open e-mails or attachments from people you don't know
5. Don't download programs from sites that look fishy

Future Fuels

Wristwatches, cell phones, clocks, and portable video game players all need energy-producing batteries to run. So do cars. But batteries store limited amounts of energy, and at some point they run down. Scientists today are working hard to find new ways to keep the energy flowing—and make sure that everything's moving smoothly.

Here Comes the Sun

With **solar cells** you'll never run out of energy on a sunny day. These devices convert sunlight into electricity that can power almost everything in your home, from a pocket calculator to your refrigerator.

Most solar cells contain a material called silicon that turns the sun's rays into electricity.

Awesome Fact

Researchers at the Massachusetts Institute of Technology (MIT), a university for scientists and engineers, know that plants have been turning sunlight into energy for billions of years. So they are experimenting with a solar cell powered by the same plant that gave Popeye *his* energy—spinach!

Cleaner Cars

If you've ever noticed what comes out of the tailpipes of cars, it may not surprise you that gasoline creates pollution. So scientists are trying to perfect **hydrogen-based** fuel cells that produce enough electricity to power a car without polluting the air. The cells have great possibilities for the future—although they're not cheap or easy to make.

One day this beauty might pass you on the road: the **FC Sport**, Honda's model of a hydrogen-powered, zero-emissions car.

NASA has been using hydrogen in the space program for years. Liquid hydrogen fuel powers NASA's space shuttles; hydrogen fuel cells run the shuttles' electrical systems.

Awesome Facts

● **Hydrogen** is the most plentiful gas in the universe. But on Earth, it's found in combinations with other elements. Water, for example, or H_2O, is a combination of two molecules of hydrogen and one of oxygen. The hydrogen must be separated from the oxygen so that it can be used as fuel.

● The United States produces enough hydrogen every year to power 20-30 million cars. One big problem: There are only about 63 hydrogen refueling stations across the country—and many more would be needed to make the switch to hydrogen-powered cars.

Pee Power

THE PROBLEM: Household batteries are difficult to get rid of because they contain harmful heavy-metal compounds that may leak into the soil and cause serious pollution.

THE SOLUTION: Pee! Scientists in the Asian nation of Singapore have figured out a way to use human urine to create a chemical reaction that recharges a basic battery. Adding a drop of pee to a group of chemicals produces as much power as an AA battery and is safer for the environment. Scientists say that more work is still needed before the batteries are ready for use by the public.

What Robots Can Do for You!

For more than 40 years, **ROBOTS** have worked in factories doing jobs too boring or too dangerous for humans. Now, new robots are starting to help humans at home, at work, at school—and even on Mars.

Welcome, Human!

Ubix, a Japanese company, has created a friendly robot known as **Ubiko**. It greets people as they walk into a store or hospital and gives directions. Ubiko is four feet four inches (1.32 m) tall, and strong enough to carry a suitcase!

Robo-Chef

If you want someone, or something, to make lunch, then China's **AIC-AI Cooking Robot** is who, or what, you need in the kitchen. AIC-AI can whip up all kinds of Chinese dishes— fried, baked, boiled or steamed! Eggroll, anyone?

Our Pal Asimo

The most popular Japanese robot, **Asimo** (*ah*-see-moh), looks like a little human in a space suit and can do lots of things that humans can do. This bot can run, climb stairs, kick a soccer ball, hold hands with its owner, and even conduct an orchestra.

Awesome Fact

Asimo stands for Advanced Step in Innovative Mobility.

TOP 5 Countries with the Most Robots

Each year, more and more robots take on tasks that people would rather not do. Robots do not mind working long hours in a factory—after all, they are machines! These are the countries with the most industrial robots.

	NUMBER OF ROBOTS
400,000	
350,000	
300,000	
250,000	
200,000	
150,000	
100,000	
50,000	
0	

Japan	U.S.	Germany	South Korea	Italy
353,300	153,630	145,200	77,300	64,500

Source: International Federation of Robotics

Splitting Water

To power cars, buses, and space shuttles with hydrogen fuel, scientists have had to figure out a way to separate hydrogen from water—or H_2O (two molecules of hydrogen and one molecule of oxygen). One process is called electrolysis. You can try it yourself in just a few minutes, with the help of a grown-up.

You Will Need

- A 9-volt battery

- Two regular number 2 pencils (remove eraser and metal part)

- One teaspoon salt

- Thin cardboard

- Electrical wire

- Small drinking glass

(1) Sharpen the pencils at both ends.

(2) Cut the cardboard to fit over the rim of the glass.

(3) Push the two pencils, about an inch apart, through the cardboard.

(4) Fill the glass half-way up with warm water.

(5) Dissolve about a teaspoon of salt into the warm water and let it sit for a while. The salt helps conduct the electricity in the water.

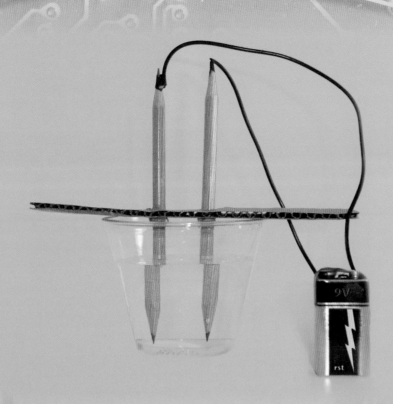

⑥ Connect one end of a piece of electrical wire to the positive side of the battery. Connect the other end of the wire to the black graphite sharp tip of one pencil. Connect another piece of wire to the negative side of the battery and to the second pencil tip.

⑦ Push the other two ends of the pencil into the water and keep your eye on the tips in the water. If you see bubbles forming, you've succeeded in splitting water into hydrogen and oxygen. Awesome!

The Science Behind It

As electricity from the battery passes through the wires and between the pencils (electrodes), the water splits into hydrogen and chlorine gas. Hydrogen bubbles form around the cathode pencil (negative end) and chlorine gas bubbles form around the anode pencil (positive end). (The chlorine comes from the salt, whose chemical formula is sodium chloride). Oxygen is not given off in this experiment. In real electrolysis systems, a different solution is used, and higher levels of electricity split the water molecules into hydrogen and oxygen without producing chlorine.

Awesome Fact

Hydrogen is the first element in the periodic table, a chart that organizes all the elements discovered so far according to their atomic mass. Hydrogen is number one because it's the lightest element, with only one proton in each hydrogen atom.

Chapter 13
The AWeSOMe Human Body

The **HUMAN BODY** is a truly awesome machine made up of many different parts that work together in extraordinary ways. In this chapter you'll discover some surprising and incredible facts about your body and the amazing things it can do.

In This Chapter

- Bacteria in Your Body
- A Helping Bionic Hand
- Awesome Eyes
- And Much More…

For the Record

There are 100 trillion (that's 100,000,000,000,000) bacteria cells in the human body, outnumbering other types of cells by 10 to one!

Awesome Fact

A healthy human eye can see millions of different colors.

Awesome Fact

High-tech software combines with human muscles to make the iLimb —a powerful prosthetic, or artificial, hand.

Awesome Fact

Think about this: The average brain thinks 70,000 thoughts per day!

Good Germs

Washing your hands before you eat helps rid them of harmful BACTERIA (back-*teer*-ee-uh), **germs that can make you sick. But did you know that most bacteria won't hurt you at all? In fact, there are trillions of bacteria in our bodies that work hard to keep us healthy.**

Bacteria in Action

About 2,000 species of bacteria—single-cell organisms—are among the oldest living creatures on Earth. Bacteria play an important role in keeping our planet in balance. They break down waste from rotting animal and plant life and turn it into water, new cells, and other organic materials that our environment needs to thrive.

Awesome Fact

Bacteria are found everywhere—in soil, in water, and in the bodies of plants and animals.

Billions of stomach bacteria break down the food we eat so that our bodies can absorb the nutrients.

Blast from the Past

Doctors had no idea that bacteria existed until 1876, when a Dutch scientist, Antonie Philips van Leeuwenhoek (*lay*-when-hook) looked through a microscope and saw tiny creatures he called "animacules." That great discovery helped later microbiologists—scientists who study microscopic lifeforms—develop medicines for diseases caused by harmful bacteria.

Awesome Fact

Bacteria create oxygen—about half of the oxygen in the atmosphere.

Six kinds of bacteria live in our inner elbow—one million of them in a patch of skin that is smaller than one square inch (about one sq cm). These bacteria keep our skin moist and healthy.

Putting Brain Power to Work

Humans have the best-developed brains in the animal kingdom. But as smart as we may be, scientists have only a rough idea of how the different parts of the **BRAIN** do what they do. Even so, we are learning more about how our brains work and how they can help people do some pretty awesome things.

The Five Parts of the Human Brain

NAME	FUNCTION
Cerebrum	Directs thinking and muscle movement
Cerebellum	Controls balance and coordination
Brain Stem	Connects to the spinal cord, which connects to the body
Pituitary	Controls body growth
Hypothalamus	Controls body temperature

cerebrum

hypothalamus

pituitary

cerebellum

brain stem

Unforgettable

A 42-year-old Los Angeles woman, Jill Price, has such a sharp memory that scientists are studying her brain. Price remembers every day of her life since the age of 14 and can tell you exactly what she was doing, say, on a certain Saturday almost 30 years ago! What researchers discover about the way Price's brain works might some day help people who have memory problems.

Brainy Action

Whenever you run to catch a ball or you jump on a bike, particular areas of your brain are working together. One area makes you remember how much you like catching balls or riding bikes. Another makes your muscles do what you want.

Awesome Facts

● Roughly 100 billion (100,000,000,000) nerve cells in our brains process our thoughts, movements, and the workings of our bodies.

● The average brain thinks 70,000 thoughts per day!

● The brain is about 3% of a person's total body weight—but uses 17% of the oxygen circulating in the body.

● When we yawn, we take in a big gulp of oxygen, which makes our brains more alert.

● You don't laugh when you tickle yourself because the cerebellum tells the rest of your body not to respond.

● Our brains are 80% water!

● Bigger isn't always better: The size of a person's brain has no relation to how smart he or she is.

iPod Brains?

Ever get a song into your head—and can't get it out for a day or so? That's normal. But some people—even if they are deaf—hear loud music inside their heads as if there were a jukebox or iPod playing pop tunes, Christmas carols, or symphonies right between their ears. Brain specialists are now studying these tricks of the mind to find out what causes them. Perhaps they will soon learn why Beethoven, a deaf composer, was able to write such beautiful music.

What an Eyeful!

The ancient Greeks had a word for it: *optikos* (*op*-tee-kos). From that we get optic, optical, optician, and optometrist. All these words relate to our **AMAZING EYES** which, after the brain, make up the most complicated organ in our bodies.

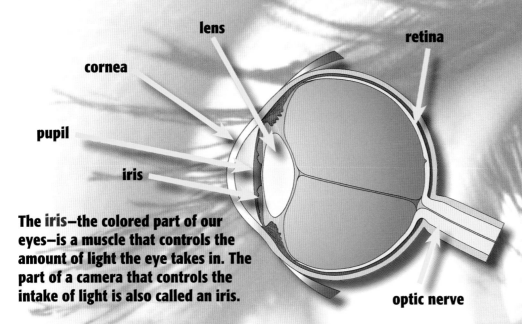

lens

cornea

pupil

iris

retina

optic nerve

The iris—the colored part of our eyes—is a muscle that controls the amount of light the eye takes in. The part of a camera that controls the intake of light is also called an iris.

The retina, a lining at the back of our eyes, contains millions of light-sensitive cells called cones (which make out colors) and rods (which help people to see in low levels of light). When light reaches the retina, it sends signals through the optic nerve to the brain. The brain then combines the signals from both eyeballs into one image.

Color Test

People who are color blind have trouble seeing certain colors. Eye doctors use a simple test, like this one, to determine color blindness. Can you see a number in the circle?

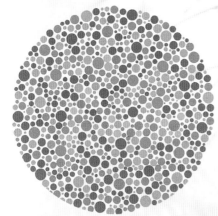

Answer: 74

Is Seeing Always Believing?

Optical illusions trick your eyes and your brain into seeing something differently from the way it really is. Here's one famous example. Do the lines in this picture look wavy? Test them with a ruler or the straight edge of a piece of paper and find out if you can believe what you see.

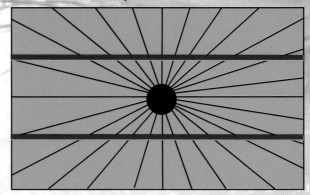

Awesome Facts

- Our eye muscles—the strongest muscles in the body—move more than 100,000 times a day.

- It's impossible to sneeze with your eyes open!

- Microscopic bacteria that live between our eyelashes and along our eyelids help protect those areas from harmful germs.

- Color-sensitive cones in the retina can tell the difference between 100 gradations of color. When the brain combines these variations, the average person can see millions of different hues.

Night Sight

Scientists are still trying to figure out exactly how animals and insects see the world. One thing they do know: Except for humans, most vertebrate animals (animals with backbones) have a tapetum (tuh-*pee*-tum). That's a kind of mirror behind the retina of their eyes. The tapetum is the reason why many animals can see clearly in the dark. The yellow glow in the eyes of a cat at night is caused by the tapetum.

Awesome Fact

Our eyes are on duty 24/7—they're working even when we're asleep. In one of the deepest phases of sleep, called Rapid Eye Movement (REM), our eyes are "seeing" our dreams.

A New Bionic Age

In *The Six Million Dollar Man*, a TV series from the 1970s, an injured astronaut is given electronic body part replacements that make him super-human. Thanks to technology, some of what that series showed is a reality today.

The Blade Runner

Oscar Pistorius lost both lower legs to a terrible bone disease when he was a baby. But that didn't stop him from enjoying rugby, water polo, and tennis as a child. With the help of artificial lower legs called Cheetahs, he has become a world-class sprinter in the Paralympics—an Olympics for physically disabled athletes.

For the Record

Pistorius, nicknamed "Blade Runner," holds the world record in the 100-, 200-, and 400-meter sprints for athletes who are disabled in one or both legs. Pistorius hopes to qualify for the Summer Olympic Games, where he would have to compete with able-bodied runners.

The remarkable Cheetah Flex-Foot is made of wood and high-strength carbon fibers, or threads.

Running without feet, ankles, or calves means that Pistorius gets most of his power from his hips and knees. He's helped by the spring-like action of the Cheetahs, which require less than half the muscle force of normal limbs in a sprinting race.

Actual Size

Helping Hand

Evan Reynolds, a British teenager, lost his left hand in a car accident. So doctors fitted him with an **iLimb**—an artificial hand with life-like fingers that are controlled by a person's mind and muscles. Equipped with the iLimb, Reynolds can once again do hundreds of things he used to take for granted— peel a potato, catch a ball, or even swing a racket.

To perform a particular movement, the iLimb obeys electrical signals sent by the user's brain to the muscles and tendons in the arm.

The iLimb's grip is strong enough to hold a heavy mug or the handle of a suitcase.

Awesome Fact

With a turn of one screw, each finger can be easily removed for repair in an iLimb clinic.

Body Basics

There are lots of fun things to learn about the **HUMAN BODY** that might come in handy for a school test or a trivia game! Here are a few fun facts to keep in mind.

Up on Bones

We need **bones** for two important reasons: They give shape and structure to our bodies, and they protect our internal organs.

The Skin We're In

Human skin, our body's largest organ, is soft, strong, and waterproof. It keeps our other body organs inside—and harmful bacteria outside—the body. Skin also repairs itself every day by shedding tens of thousands of old, dried-out cells.

Awesome Fact

Over a lifetime, most people cast off about 40 pounds (18 kg) of skin. In fact, more than half of the dust you see in your house is made of shed skin!

Awesome Fact

At birth, people have more than 300 bones. But by the time they reach adulthood, they'll have just 206—because some bones fuse, or connect to each other, as we grow.

Muscle Mania

Muscles allow us to move by pulling and pushing our skeleton along. Some muscles, like the heart, are involuntary. That means they work on their own. Others are voluntary. We make voluntary muscles move by doing something, such as reaching for an apple or turning the page of a book.

Awesome Fact

Our largest muscle is the one we sit on: the gluteus maximus (*glue*-tee-us *max*-uh-muss)—the Latin term for your bottom.

Tasteful Tongues

Next time you stick out your **tongue**, remember that it is made up of many groups of muscles. Coating the tongue is a layer of sensors that feel heat, pain, and other sensations. Among these sensors are about 10,000 taste buds—little bumps made of receptor cells that tell your brain whether the food you're eating is sweet, salty, sour, bitter, or savory. There are about 50-100 receptor cells in each taste bud.

Can you curl or fold your tongue? Many people can!

Awesome Fact

If you burn your tongue with a very hot slice of pizza, don't worry; the tongue grows new receptor cells every one to two weeks.

Tongue Twister

When we speak, the movement of tongue muscles helps us produce a range of sounds. That's why a sequence of sounds that is difficult to say is called a tongue twister. Try to keep track of what your tongue is doing when you say this tongue twister five times, really fast (if you can).
Round the rugged rocks the rapid rabbit ran!

Chapter 14
AweSoMe History

We have thousands of years of human history behind us, and billions of years of natural history before that. By looking back, we learn so much about where we've come from and how we got to where we are today. And we can use past history lessons to help guide us into the future.

Awesome Fact

From the 8th to the 11th century, fierce VIKINGS from Scandinavia sailed away in their sturdy oak longboats to raid villages in the British Isles and Europe. Because they were excellent navigators, the Vikings also succeeded in crossing the Atlantic and reaching Iceland, Greenland, and parts of the North American coast.

In This Chapter

- Sailors Before Columbus
- A Little League Wonder
- Explorers in Space
- And Much More...

The first person to go over Niagara Falls in a barrel was **ANNIE TAYLOR**, a Michigan schoolteacher, in 1901. She was 63 years old!

ANNIE EDSON TAYLOR
HEROINE OF NIAGARA FALLS
OCT 24 1901
F.M. RUSSELL Mgr.

Awesome Fact

Lots of people thought he was crazy, but **ROBERT GODDARD** knew exactly what he was doing. He was the first person in history to launch a liquid fueled rocket, on March 16, 1926.

Hers
Leaders in History

We take for granted that American girls go to school, play sports, and aim for any career they choose, including running for President of the United States. But here's an awesome fact: Less than 100 years ago, the U.S. Constitution did not give women the right to vote. Women won that right because they fought for it—and have fought for other civil rights, as well.

Girl at Bat

In 1950, only boys could be on Little League baseball teams. That was a problem for **Kathryn Johnston**, a 12-year-old from Corning, New York, who was a good baseball player. Kathryn tried out for Little League disguised as a boy named "Tubby" (her favorite character from an old comic strip) and made the team! When she later told her secret to the coach, he decided to let her stay. Still, in 1951, Little League officials made a rule: NO GIRLS! It wasn't until 1974 that a court ruling opened a New Jersey Little League team to girls—and made the national organization change its policy.

Johnston in 2010

For the Record

More than 5 million girls have played Little League baseball and softball since they were allowed to participate in 1974.

FIGHTING FOR WOMEN'S RIGHTS

American history books are filled with stories of amazing women who spent their entire lives trying to win equal rights for females.

Susan B. Anthony (1820-1906) and Elizabeth Stady Canton (1815-1902) Activists who organized a movement to fight for women's suffrage, or the right to vote

Mary McLeod Bethune (1875-1955) African-American educator and civil rights leader who brought together several black women's groups to try to end racism and job discrimination against African Americans

Patsy Mink (1927-2002) First Asian-American woman to win a seat in Congress (1964) and a worker for education, childcare, and a clean environment

Dolores Huerta (1930-) Hispanic-American labor union organizer who fought for decent wages and living conditions for U.S. farm workers

Famous Female Firsts in U.S. History

1766-1777 Mary Catherine Goddard First woman publisher in the American colonies, first woman to run a city postal system, first printer to publish a copy of the Declaration of Independence with the names of the signers

1848 First women's rights convention held in U.S. at Seneca Falls, NY

1849 Dr. Elizabeth Blackwell First woman to earn a medical degree

1869 Arabella Mansfield First woman lawyer

1869 Formation of National Women's Suffrage Association to fight for voting rights

1872 Victoria Woodhull First woman to run for President

1920 19th Amendment to U.S. Constitution, giving women the right to vote, signed into law

1924 Nellie Ross First woman to serve as state governor (Wyoming)

1932 Amelia Earhart First woman to fly alone across the Atlantic

1935 National Council of Negro Women organized to fight racism and job discrimination

1946 Edith Houghton First woman hired as a major-league baseball scout

1963 Congress passes equal pay act, requiring women be paid same wages as men for same job

1969 Shirley Chisholm First African-American woman elected to Congress

1970 Diane Crump First female jockey to ride in the Kentucky Derby

1981 Sandra Day O'Connor First woman U.S. Supreme Court Justice

1983 Sally Ride First American woman in space

1985 Wilma Mankiller First woman Chief of the Cherokee Nation (Oklahoma)

1990 Dr. Antonia Novello First woman sworn in as U.S. Surgeon General, the nation's chief doctor

1997 Madeleine Albright First woman Secretary of State

2007 Dr. Peggy Whitson first woman to command International Space Station

Move Over, Columbus!

Christopher Columbus gets a lot of attention—and a national holiday—in the United States. But when he landed on the island of San Salvador in 1492, he was only the latest in a long line of explorers who risked their lives to find new worlds.

The ruins of Tharros, a city founded by Phoenicians, are still to be seen in what is now Sardinia.

c. 1000 B.C. **PHOENICIANS**, people living in city-states along the Mediterranean (now modern Syria, Israel, and Lebanon), send ships to find trading partners in Egypt, Greece, parts of Spain, and Africa

1000-800 B.C. **GREEK** explorers settle around the Mediterranean, including Turkey, southern Italy, Sicily, and Persia (modern Iran)

1000 B.C. **SAILORS** from Indonesia and parts of Southeast Asia begin to explore the Pacific Ocean in simple canoes and to settle on chains of islands in the South Pacific that were later called Polynesia

356-323 B.C. **ALEXANDER THE GREAT**, King of Macedonia, conquers Persia, and reaches Egypt, Central Asia, Afghanistan, and India

172-114 B.C. **CHANG CH'IEN**, a Chinese explorer, travels as far west as Samarkand and Uzbekistan in Asia, creating a "Silk Road" for trade between China and the Roman Empire

Xian (see-*ann*) is a walled city in central China. It once bordered the Silk Road, a famous trading route.

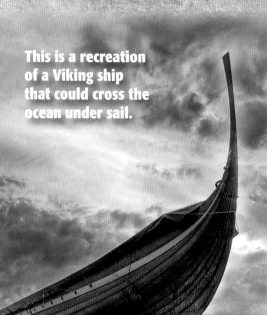

This is a recreation of a Viking ship that could cross the ocean under sail.

700-1000 A.D. **THE VIKINGS**, a seafaring people from Scandinavia, explore Iceland, Greenland, Newfoundland, and part of North America's Atlantic coast

1271-1295 **MARCO POLO** travels throughout Asia, from Turkey to China, then writes about it in *The Book of Marco Polo*, an important guide for explorers such as Columbus

1333-1364 **IBN BATTUTA**, an Arab explorer from Morocco, spends 31 years traveling to places in the Islamic world, as well as India, China, and Bulgaria

1444-1446 **PRINCE HENRY** of Portugal develops the caravel, a light-weight, fast-moving ship that carries Portuguese explorers along the coast of Africa

1492 **CHRISTOPHER COLUMBUS** lands in San Salvador

These are replicas of Columbus's famous sailing ships, the *Niña*, the *Pinta*, and the *Santa Maria*.

Beyond Planet Earth

Since the early 20th century, there have been many landmark "firsts" in the race to explore outer space. While some of the most amazing space trips have been piloted by humans, unmanned spacecraft and probes have done their part, sending back awesome photographs of places we have yet to visit.

Rocket Science

On March 16, 1926, Robert H. Goddard, a U.S. scientist, launched the first liquid fueled rocket in history from his aunt's Massachusetts farm. Called "Nell," the four-foot-high rocket went 41 feet (12 m) in the air and flew for just 2½ seconds. But Goddard was pleased, even though lots of folks called him "Moony" because he dreamed of sending rockets to the moon. Years later, after many experiments, Goddard worked out the basics of rocket technology. When he died in 1945, he left behind detailed records that helped younger rocket scientists make those moon-dreams a reality.

Awesome Fact

In a famous speech on May 25, 1961, President John F. Kennedy declared: "...I believe that this nation should commit itself to achieving the goal, before this decade is out, of landing a man on the moon and returning him safely to the Earth." Eight years later, *Apollo 11* accomplished Kennedy's goal.

Space Exploration Highlights

THE MOON July 1969 – American astronauts Neil Armstrong and Edwin ("Buzz") Aldrin, Jr. of the *Apollo 11* mission become the first humans to set foot on the moon.

MERCURY By March 2011, NASA's *Messenger* spacecraft, the second to visit Mercury, is scheduled to begin orbiting the planet.

VENUS December 1970 – The Soviet Union's probe, *Venera 7*, lands here, becoming the first spacecraft to land on another planet and send data back to Earth.

EARTH October 1957 – The USSR (the Soviet Union) launches the world's first artificial satellite, *Sputnik 1*. Each orbit of the Earth takes about 96 minutes.

MARS July and September 1976 – America's *Viking 1* and *Viking 2* land probes on Mars that send back the first pictures of the Red Planet.

JUPITER March and July 1979 – U.S. *Voyager 1* and *Voyager 2* approach Jupiter and send back pictures of the enormous planet and its moons.

SATURN July 2004 – After seven years of space travel, the U.S. *Cassini* probe begins orbiting the planet and discovers its rings are made mostly of reddish ice.

NEPTUNE August 1989 – *Voyager 2* is the first spacecraft to observe Neptune, passing about 3,000 miles (4,950 km) above its north pole.

URANUS January 1986 – *Voyager 2* flies close to Uranus and radios back huge amounts of data and thousands of photographs.

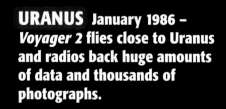

Chapter 15
Awesome Mysteries

Awesome Fact

Since 1934, hundreds of people claim to have spotted a prehistoric monster swimming in Scotland's LOCH NESS.

In ancient times, everyone thought that the mighty god Zeus threw thunderbolts from the heavens. It was a great story—but now we know the science behind the bolt. The world is still full of weird sights and events that scientists have yet to explain.

Awesome Fact

The BERMUDA TRIANGLE , an area of the Atlantic Ocean, is supposed to be a place where numerous airplanes and ships vanish without a trace.

In This Chapter

Awesome Fact

Peru's **NAZCA LINES** —70 ancient earth drawings scattered over hundreds of miles—can only be seen from an airplane or helicopter.

Awesome Fact

England's **STONEHENGE**, one of the most famous stone circles in the world, dates back to 3100 B.C.

Strange Sightings

From time to time, people report seeing weird creatures in the woods or mysterious objects in the sky. These sightings may be tricks of light and shadow or the creations of strong imaginations. Whatever the reason for them, these visions have inspired legends, campfire tales, and scary movies!

Is It a Bird? Is It a Plane?

Or is it a **UFO**—an unidentified flying object? UFOs are exactly that: objects we see in the sky but can't quite recognize. That doesn't stop millions of people around the globe from believing that every UFO is a spaceship carrying aliens from another planet or galaxy.

Nessie of the Loch

Her nickname is "Nessie." But she's mostly known as the **Loch Ness Monster**: a dinosaur-like creature that is said to lurk in the dark waters of a loch, or lake, in Scotland. For years, after a local doctor claimed to have snapped her photo in 1934, thousands insisted that they saw her, too. Does she exist? To answer that question, a British team searched the loch with sonar (sound-detecting instruments) in 2003. Sadly, no Nessie.

Big Tracks in the Snow

Years ago, in the U.S. Pacific Northwest, a few people reported finding huge and not-quite-human footprints in the snow. Some took photos or plaster casts of these mysterious tracks, claiming they were made by giant, ape-like creatures that live in the woods. Ever since, others have declared that they, too, have seen "**Bigfoot**" tracks—and sometimes, Bigfoot itself. But scientists say that the reports and photos are fakes. Could it be that the story of Bigfoot is a new twist on the old Tibetan myth of the Abominable Snowman?

INCHES 1

Actual Size

A Pyramid or a Calendar?

It's both! The **Kukulkan Pyramid**, on the Yucatan peninsula in Mexico, is the legacy of the mysterious Mayan Empire that flourished in Central America more than a thousand years ago. Many people who live in Mexico, Guatemala, and other parts of Central America today are descendants of the Mayas and still speak a form of their language.

The temple is dedicated to the Mayan god Kukulkan, the Feathered Serpent.

Awesome Fact

Twice a year, when the sun sets on the evening of the first day of spring and the first day of fall, a shadow resembling the snake-god Kukulkan slithers down the northern stairway.

Stone sculptures of the serpent god run down the sides of the northern staircase.

A doorway leads to a dark staircase and a mysterious shrine with a Jaguar throne.

Awesome Fact

The Mayas built a powerful civilization long before Christopher Columbus landed in the New World. Their knowledge of writing, astronomy and mathematics helped them to erect beautiful cities and create an accurate system of calendars.

4 x 91 = 364 + 1 = 365

Kukulkan is actually a solar calendar! Each of its four sides has a stairway with 91 steps. Multiply 4 x 91, add the platform at the top, and you get 365! On each side, there are nine terraces divided into 18 parts—one for each month of the Mayan year.

Ring of Mystery

In the Anglo-Saxon language—an early form of English— STONEHENGE means "hanging stones." But the stone pillars of Stonehenge, on a vast plain in southern England, don't hang at all. Instead, the ancient stones are set firmly upright in two concentric circles—circles with a common center. Who put them there and for what purpose are mysteries we may never be able to solve.

In 3100 B.C., ancient Britons most likely began the first work at Stonehenge. They may have used deer antlers to dig a deep, circular ditch with a diameter of 320 feet (98 m). The stones were put in place, in stages, much later on—sometime between 2100 B.C. and 1100 B.C.

Many experts believe that Stonehenge was a place of worship and burial. Others say Stonehenge reflects its makers' understanding of astronomy because it lines up with sunrise, sunset, and moonrise at key points during the changing seasons.

The pillars are made of two types of stone. **Bluestones**, which could weigh up to 8,000 pounds (3,629 kg) each, were most likely taken from a stone quarry 240 miles (384 km) away. **Sarsen stones**, carried about 20 miles to the site, were as long as 30 feet (9.1 m) and could weigh up to 100,000 pounds (45,359 kg) each.

Awesome Facts

● Contrary to popular belief, Stonehenge was not built by Druid priests. The Druids were part of a Celtic culture that flourished a thousand years or so after the stone ring was created.

● One legend has it that Stonehenge was built by the great wizard **Merlin**, who brought the mighty pillars from Ireland with the help of giants and magic.

A rendering of ancient Stonehenge showing the concentric circles

The Puzzling Nazca Lines

The Nazca desert of Peru is one of the driest places on Earth—and also one of the most surprising. Up close it looks like a reddish, pebbly strip of land. But if you hop on board a small plane and take to the air, you can see huge earth drawings, or geoglyphs, and 800 intersecting lines, triangles, and spirals laid out for miles on the stony desert floor! Who drew these Nazca Lines? What was their purpose? How were they created? There are lots of theories—but nobody really knows the answers.

Seventy drawings that can only be seen from the air are scattered over an area of more than 200 square miles (520 sq km). The most famous are the monkey, the spider, the condor, and the hummingbird. There is also a human figure that looks like an astronaut!

The lines are thought to have been made by Nazca people who lived in the area between 200 B.C. and 700 A.D. They also left behind beautiful pottery and traces of an advanced irrigation system to water their crops.

The **Spider** is 150 feet (45 m) long and drawn in one continuous line. It is a type of spider found only in the Amazon rain forest—hundreds of miles away! Scholars wonder how the Nazca people knew about it.

The Nazcas moved pebbles on the desert surface to make the drawings. But without airplanes or other means of rising above the earth, how could they draw such huge images in such perfect scale?

The width of each line varies. Some are no more than a few feet across, about the size of a footpath. The lines range in width from 16 inches (40 cm) to 3.6 feet (1.10 m).

Now You See It, Now You Don't

When magicians make rabbits and doves vanish into thin air, we know it's a trick. But throughout history, there have been tales of unsolved human disappearances that we're still puzzling over.

Gone Missing?

Whether they call it the **Bermuda Triangle** or the Devil's Triangle, many people believe this 500,000 square mile (1,294,994 sq km) area of the Atlantic Ocean is a place where numerous airplanes and ships have mysteriously vanished. Most people say it's as safe to travel through the Triangle as any other part of the Atlantic.

NORTH AMERICA

Awesome Facts

● Believers in the paranormal—events that science cannot explain—say that more than 2,000 ships and 75 airplanes have disappeared over the Bermuda Triangle in the last 300 years. But skeptics say that most of the statistics about the Triangle are either wrong or simply made up.

● The story goes that Christopher Columbus passed through the Triangle in 1492 and reported seeing strange dancing lights and flames in the sky. Still, he made it safely through the area and found his way to the shores of the New World.

Inside the walls of tall cliffs in Colorado, the Anasazi carved out a labyrinth of homes, religious centers, storehouses, and reservoirs—even, in one location, a five-story "apartment house" with 800 rooms!

A Truly Lost Civilization

Sometime around 1200 B.C., an ancient American Indian people called the Anasazi (ah-nuh-*sah*-zee) settled in different parts of the southwestern United States. Although they had no writing systems, they were awesome builders. Near the end of the 13th century, the Anasazi completely abandoned their cities. Experts are still trying to figure out why.

You can still visit the cities the Anasazi left behind, like this one at Mesa Verde National Monument in Colorado.

Index

Photo Credits

All photos clockwise from top left, unless indicated otherwise

Key: (S) = Shutterstock, b = background image

Cover: EugeneF (S); Giuseppe R (fingers) (S); SoleilC (S); Andreas Meyer (S)

Back cover: NASA; Monkey Business Images (S); INNOCENt (S)

p 3: Brooke Whatnall (S); Robert Zehner (S); Bonnie Lee Kellogg/©iStockphoto.com

pp 4-5: Peter Weber (S); Courtesy of Mike Buckley, Boys Town; Dennis Klimov (S); Creations (S); Danilo Ascione (S); Vulkanette (S); NASA

pp 6-7: John Whitley-Gibson; Joy Strotz (S); Kanadier; Kanadier; Akhilesh (S); Matthew Jacques (S); public domain; Robert King (S); Courtesy of Kay Massar; Ianafloat (S); Viktar Malyshchyts (S); b: PILart

pp 8-9: KENCKO photography (S); Rcragun; Brooke Whatnall (S); b: Vera Volkova (S)

pp 10-11: Andreas Meyer (S); SkullsUnlimited.com; Jaimie Duplass (S)

pp 12-13: Dr. Morley Read (S); fivespots (S); Brooke Whatnall (S)

pp 14-15: Eric Isselée (S); Nagel Photography (S); ncn18 (S); Eric Isselée (S); Lerche & Johnson (S); b: ncn18 (S)

pp 16-17: From top to bottom: Gary Blakeley (S); Carmen Ruiz (S); Robert Zehner (S); EugeneF (S); KENCKO photography (S); b: Vera Volkova (S)

pp 18-19: All photos courtesy of Singapore Flyer/Adval Brand Group Pte Ltd

pp 20-21: Wagaung (2 Kuthodaw Pagoda photos); Dottie Stover/University of Cincinnati; b: Matt Antonino (S)

pp 22-23: kiselilimun (S); Mark A. Wilson (Department of Geology, The College of Wooster); Free Soul Production (S); Giuseppe R (fingers) (S); SoleilC (S); b: kentoh (S)

pp 24-25: Koekeloer (S); Jonathan Larsen (S); Koekeloer (S)

pp 26-27: Courtesy Jay Shafer, Tumbleweed Tiny House Company; Caters News Agency/Rex Features; Southwest News Service/Rex Features; David Burner/Rex Features; b: Euro Color Creative (S)

pp 28-29: SF photo (S); Bill Perry (S); b: SF photo (S)

pp 30-31: Rcragun; Jim Stem, courtesy of The John and Mable Ringling Museum of Art

pp 32-33: Granger Collection, NY; NASA; INNOCENt (S); b: CLM (S)

pp 34-35: The Granger Collection, NY; public domain; public domain; b: CLM (S); INNOCENt (S); b: CLM (S)

pp 36-37: public domain; NASA; Kheng Guan Toh (S); Rokits XPrize Gallery; b: Voronin76 (S)

pp 38-39: Bonnie Lee Kellogg/©iStockphoto.com; Flip Nicklin/Minden Pictures; Alan Crosthwaite/©iStockphoto.com; Francesco Vitali; b: Olga Khoroshunova (S)

pp 40-41: Chuang Zhao and Linda Xing/AFP; Fruitadens: © The Dinosaur Institute at the Natural History Museum of Los Angeles County. Artist: Doyle Trankina; Ben2

pp 42-43: Maridav (S); Catherine Scott/©iStockphoto.com; Antoine Beyeler (S); cenker atila (S); b: Steve Herrmann (S)

pp 44-45: Luis Padilla/©iStockphoto.com; Michael Quinton/Minden Pictures; Awei (S); James Peragine (S); Jean-Paul Ferrero/Minden Pictures; b: Vera Volkova (S)

pp 46-47: Francesco Vitali; Eric Isselée (S); Steven Russell Smith Photos (S); orionmystery@flickr (S); Tom Grundy (S); b: Olga Khoroshunova (S)

pp 48-49: Norbert Wu/Minden Pictures; Michael Stubblefield/©iStockphoto.com; Norbert Wu/Minden Pictures; b: Sergey Popov V (S)

pp 50-51: © Nancy Nehring/©iStockphoto.com; photonimo/©iStockphoto.com; © Peter Wey/©iStockphoto.com; © Cynthia Lindow/©iStockphoto.com; b: zimmytws (S)

pp 52-53: Bolt: Pete Niesen (S); photobar (S); Michael J Thompson (S); Hedrus (S); lsantilli (S); Mogens Trolle (S); niall dunne (S)

pp 54-55: Elephants: Zastol`skiy Victor Leonidovich (S); Peter Kirillov (S); John A. Anderson (S); Gelpi (S)

pp 56-57: Steve Herrmann (S); OSU; cbpix (S); Peter Radacsi (S); b: Olga Khoroshunova (S)

pp 58-59: Katherine Moffitt/©iStockphoto.com; Krivosheev Vitaly (S); Grigoryeva Liubov Dmitrievna (S); Lori Martin (S); Greg Cerenzio (S); b: Patsy Michaud (S)

pp 60-61: John R Smith (S); David Quixley (S); b: Nagy Melinda (S)

pp 62-63: S.Borisov (S); aliola (S); xjbxjhxm123 (S); Lagui (S); b: Nagy Melinda (S)

pp 64-65: Nancy Nehring/©iStockphoto.com; Matthijs Wetterauw (S); Jonathan Maddock/©iStockphoto.com; b: Mary Lane

pp 66-67: ooyoo/©iStockphoto.com; Lacy Rane/©iStockphoto.com; Lamp Lighter SDV (S); Rick Szczechowski/©iStockphoto.com; V.Shvydkova (S); Bryan Faust/©iStockphoto.com

pp 68-69: Karin Hildebrand Lau (S); Andrey Yurlov (S); Ben Haslam/Haslam Photography (S); public domain; b: Andrey Yurlov (S)

pp 70-71: NatalieJean (S); Brian Finestone (S); NatalieJean (S); Joy Strotz (S); NatalieJean (S)

pp 72-73: Peter Weber (S); John Kershner (S); Olga Besnard (S); DeanHarty (S)

pp 74-75: Marcel Jancovic (S); ygor (S); Rafael Martin-Gaitero;(S); afaizal (S); De Visu (S); testing (S); J. Henning Buchholz (S); b: PILart

pp 76-77: Photo File-Hulton Archive/ Getty Images; John G. Mabanglo-AFP/Getty Images; public domain; Getty Images; Tony Duffy/Getty Images; b: Mike Liu (S)

pp 78-79: Vitalii Nesterchuk (S); Monkey Business Images (S); Philip Lange (S); public domain; Xof711 (S); b: public domain

pp 80-81: kojoku (S); public domain; public domain; White House (Joyce N. Boghosian); Laurie Barr (S); b: Alex Valent (S)

pp 82-83: public domain; public domain; frantisekhojdysz (S); Pool/Getty Images; Kapu (S); b: J. Helgason (S)

AWESOME-And Then Some!

Main Entry: AWE·SOME

Pronunciation: /*awwwwwww-sum*/

Function: *Adjective*

Date: 1598

1: filled with awe

2: inspiring awe

AND ALSO:

Amazing

Astonishing

Astounding

Breathtaking

Dazzling

Dumbfounding

Excellent

Extraordinary

Eye-popping

Formidable

Gob-smacking

Impressive

Incredible

Jaw-dropping

Kewl!

Magnificent

Marvelous

Mind-boggling

Outstanding

Remarkable

Startling

Stunning

Stupefying

Surprising

Terrific

Way cool

Wonderful

Wondrous

JUST AWESOME!